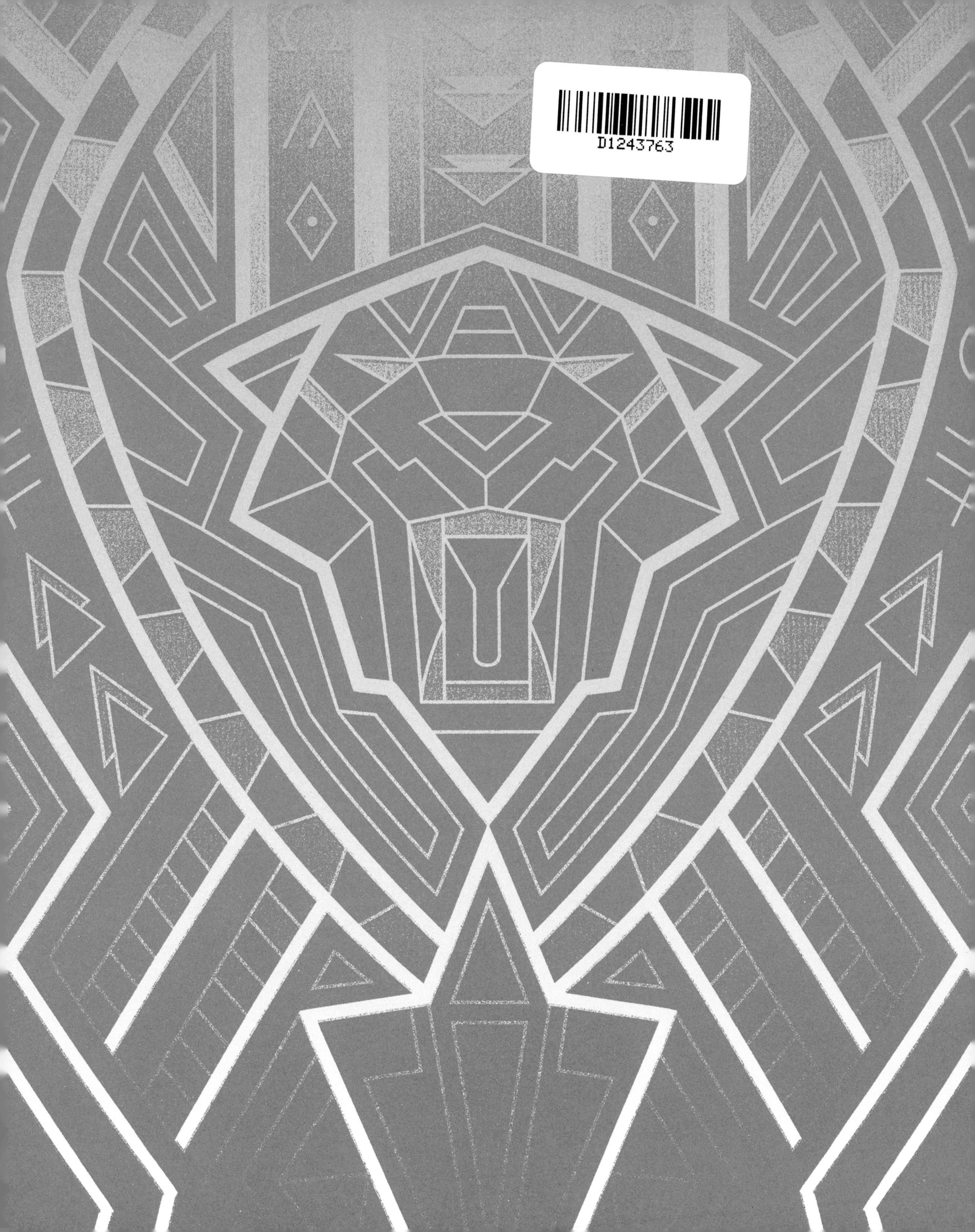

MARVEL

BLACK PANTHER

WAKANDA ATLAS

Written by
Evan Narcisse

CONTENTS

INTRODUCTION

You'd never know it from the book you're holding in your hand, but the country of Wakanda has grown immensely over the last 56 years.

When the Black Panther and his hidden African homeland first appeared in 1966 in *Fantastic Four* #52, Wakanda looked and felt a lot smaller. In that first appearance, Wakanda was primarily shown as an exoticized, unindustrialized realm. The advanced technology that's been the country's hallmark was in evidence, but readers were given the impression that the majority of the populace held more closely to traditionally agrarian ways of life.

As time passed, stories set in Wakanda tended to happen in either Central Wakanda or its more remote outlying regions. Central Wakanda was shown as an urbanized epicenterwhere technological development and interface with the outside world rippled out from the Royal Palace. The smaller villages, often portrayed as unnamed clusters of huts, were places to be protected from external threats.

Since its debut, Wakanda has moved all over Africa. It's been placed in the central region of the continent, in West Africa bordering Nigeria, and nestled in the horn of East Africa amongst Kenya, Sudan, and Uganda. But, even as the location of the nation shifted in Marvel Comics' fiction, Wakanda became more real and fleshed out in other ways. Specific regions were shown to have their own subcultures, priorities, and histories. Locales like the Jabari Mountains or the Upanga military barracks roiled with their own internal dramas of dogma and betrayal, becoming much more than mere backdrops.

Wakanda's been a lot of different things in a lot of different places. As the evolution of the country proceeded throughout the decades, the symbolism of the Unconquered Realm and the depth of its possibilities grew more and more. This book is an attempt to document and synthesize the work of hundreds of writers, artists, and editors who've crafted stories about the Black Panther and Wakanda over the years. Those stories of political turmoil and cosmic insurrection have focused on heroes and villains, but they've also made the countrysides, cityscapes, and exoplanets of the realm as rich and layered as the characters who fought in them.

So, dive in, dear reader. Learn about Serpent Valley and its fearsome dinosaurs, the mystical Wellspring of Power pulsing in the Jabari-Lands, and the secret pockets of sentient vibranium lurking across the landscape. While you're doing that, remember that Wakanda has always been a nation where change brings power and peril. It's a place where anything can happen, and its only true borders are those of the imagination.

Evan Narcisse

Notes from the illustrators

My first real introduction to the world of Wakanda was through the 2018 Black Panther movie where I was captivated by the story and the visuals, which led me to exploring and falling in love with the comics. It's been a dream come true to help capture the world of Wakanda, especially that of the Wakandan School for Alternative Studies. I was given creative freedom to design a space that captured both the futuristic sci-fi elements of Wakanda alongside the more traditional patterns and weapons that are so seamlessly combined in the comics. I hope I did it justice!

Bex Glendining (Wakandan School for Alternative Studies, p26; Galaxies of the Intergalactic Empire, p84)

Researching the map took me down the historical archives of Wakanda's portrayal. During those decades, the story of the Black Panther has grown and matured, and Wakanda has evolved with it. From more of a background setting, Wakanda has developed into a shining example of Afro-futuristic world-building with its geography, politics, and history, which underpin the Black Panther stories and give them the richness and depth we all know so well. Questions about power, society, and heroism have become integral to the locations. That is why I wished to bring realism to the map's logic while simultaneously celebrating the artwork of the previous generations of artists and writers. The map in the book is not a reinterpretation but another small piece of the expanding world of Wakanda that would hopefully help you explore its culture and history in depth.

Teo Georgiev (Wakanda map, p12, p40)

My first experience drawing the Black Panther was for "Black Panther: The Man Without Fear" published by Marvel Comics. Oddly enough in this story, T'Challa was based in New York City. Being a native of "the concrete jungle," I relished the opportunity to draw the noble king navigating this gritty, urban environment. However, since my chapters of the story were primarily set in New York, the chance to draw the legendary country of the Black Panther's birth did not come to pass. Ten years later and following the blockbuster first film, this book has finally provided me the opportunity to visualize Wakanda in all its glory. From the eclectic vibrancy of the Birnin Street Market to the vastness of the vibranium mines, to the grandeur of the Wakandan embassy, I was inspired by various elements of African culture to depict the hidden, futuristic city. Sometimes, good things come to those who wait.

Shawn Martinbrough (Birnin Zana Marketplace, p52; Vibranium Mines, p62; Inside the Wakandan Embassy, p76; colors by Adriano Lucas)

KEY CHARACTERS

T'CHALLA

The latest in a long line of rulers going back centuries, T'Challa is the Black Panther—a title that denotes him as king of Wakanda. To become the Black Panther, an aspirant must emerge victorious from ritual combat, defeating all other contenders. For this reason, the vast majority of the nation regards Black Panther as the living symbol of the realm's history, achievement, and warrior spirit. A genius-level scientist and strategist, T'Challa will best be remembered for his fateful decision to reveal Wakanda's existence and establish geopolitical relations with the world at large. Whether he's fighting alongside his teammates in the Avengers or grappling with challenges within his country's borders, King T'Challa is without a doubt one of the greatest monarchs to ever rule Wakanda.

SHURI

Shuri is T'Challa's younger half-sister, the daughter of the late King T'Chaka and his second wife Queen Ramonda. Her sheer intelligence rivals that of her brother and actually exceeds his in certain areas of study. Shuri has adopted the mantle of Black Panther in times of crisis, becoming a hero in her own brash and inimitable style.

QUEEN MOTHER RAMONDA

As a young woman, Ramonda left her native South Africa in search of resources that might help the fight against the racist apartheid regime that oppressed Black people. Her travels inadvertently brought her to Wakanda, where she helped a lost Prince T'Challa reunite with his father, King T'Chaka. T'Chaka and Ramonda fell in love and she became the king's second wife, raising T'Challa and giving birth to Shuri. Ramonda disappeared from T'Challa's life for years after she was abducted during a visit back home to South Africa, but was eventually rescued by him after he became Black Panther. Since then, she's been the strong foundation of the nation's royal family, helping guide Wakanda through every challenge it has faced.

STORM

Ororo Munroe is the child of an African-American photojournalist and a Kenyan princess who lived in Egypt. After a plane crash took the lives of her parents, Ororo became a pickpocket who stole on the streets of Cairo. She traveled south to Kenya as a teenager and used her newly manifested powers of weather manipulation to help battle drought in the Serengeti Plains. Her actions led to her being worshipped as a goddess but, eventually, she joined the X-Men super hero team to help fight for mutant rights under the code name Storm. Prior to joining the X-Men, she met Prince T'Challa when they were both still teenagers. When the two crossed paths again as adults, romance bloomed and they married. Ororo became queen of Wakanda and helped protect the realm against its enemies. Her marriage to T'Challa dissolved during a cosmic mutant crisis, but they still have great affection toward each other and Storm still aids Wakanda in times of need.

KILLMONGER

Arguably T'Challa's greatest nemesis, the man who would become Erik Killmonger was born as N'Jadaka in a small village in rural Wakanda. After his family died during an invasion raid, young N'Jadaka was kidnapped and taken into the outside world. The indignities he suffered while growing up away from his homeland hardened N'Jadaka's heart and perverted his understanding of the Wakandan ideal, spurring him to change his name. As he came of age, Killmonger vowed to return to Wakanda and take control of the nation that had seemingly abandoned him. Unaware of Killmonger's secret anger, T'Challa brought his lost countryman to Wakanda. Since then, Killmonger has led several murderous campaigns to kill the Black Panther and seize control of the nation's leadership. He has died and come back to life multiple times in pursuit of this goal, making him one of Wakanda's most implacable foes.

ZENZI

Zenzi's life began in Niganda, a war-torn nation that is Wakanda's neighbor along its southeast border. During her childhood, Killmonger's troops murdered entire villages as part of a bloody march across the land. When a young Zenzi found herself facing certain death at gunpoint, her latent powers of emotional manipulation and amplification manifested suddenly. She used these powers to make her would-be killers turn on each other and went underground. Years later, she joined forces with Wakandan rebel sorcerer Tetu to help foment a violent anti-monarchy uprising in Wakanda. Zenzi escaped capture when Tetu's gambit failed and became an unpredictable enemy to Black Panther.

TETU

Once a promising political science student in the nation's higher educational system, Tetu abandoned his studies and retreated into the wilderness for a deeper understanding of Wakanda. He focused on mastering magical abilities that let him manipulate fundamental forces of nature. Tetu became embittered at Wakanda's leadership after external cosmic warfare took the lives of millions, and he started a violent revolutionary movement called the People. Tetu and the People sought to abolish the Wakandan monarchy and waged war against King T'Challa, Princess Shuri, and their allies. Tetu was jailed after Black Panther and other Wakandan heroes thwarted the People's Revolution, but the insurgent shaman later resurfaced to bring chaos back to the Wakanda, the "Unconquered Realm."

KLAW

Born in Belgium to a German Nazi Commander whose plane crashed in Wakanda, Ulysses S. Klaw grew up hearing about vibranium and the nation's wondrous technology. The younger Klaw studied Applied Sonics at university and eventually ventured to Wakanda to try and claim vibranium for his experiments. When he was refused access to the metal, he and his mercenary forces attempted to force their way into the country. Klaw managed to kill King T'Chaka in the ensuing battle but retreated when a young T'Challa used the interloper's own sonic cannon to destroy Klaw's right hand. Years later, Klaw returned to Wakanda and again suffered defeat at the hands of an adult T'Challa—who bore the title of Black Panther—and the Fantastic Four. This encounter ended with Klaw leaping into a massive sonic converter device, which transformed him into a being composed of pure sound. Klaw became a powerful supervillain with his newfound abilities and has been a recurring threat to T'Challa and Wakanda over the years.

WAKANDA

Hidden for hundreds of generations before King T'Challa revealed its existence to the world, Wakanda is the most technologically advanced nation on Earth, boasting achievements and creations that seem impossible to imagine. Wakanda is also Earth's sole source for vibranium, an extraterrestrial metal that can absorb and project different forms of vibration and energy.

"DON'T YOU SEE? THE MIRACLE IS WAKANDA. THE MIRACLE IS ALL AROUND US."

— T'Challa

Jabari-
Lands
MOHANNDA
Birnin T'Chaka
Warrior
Falls
Birnin
Djata
Birnin Bashenga
Serpent
Valley
Mena Ngai
(The Great
Mound)
CANAAN
N'Jadaka
Village
Birnin
Azzaria
AZANIA
Mute
Zones
N
W
S

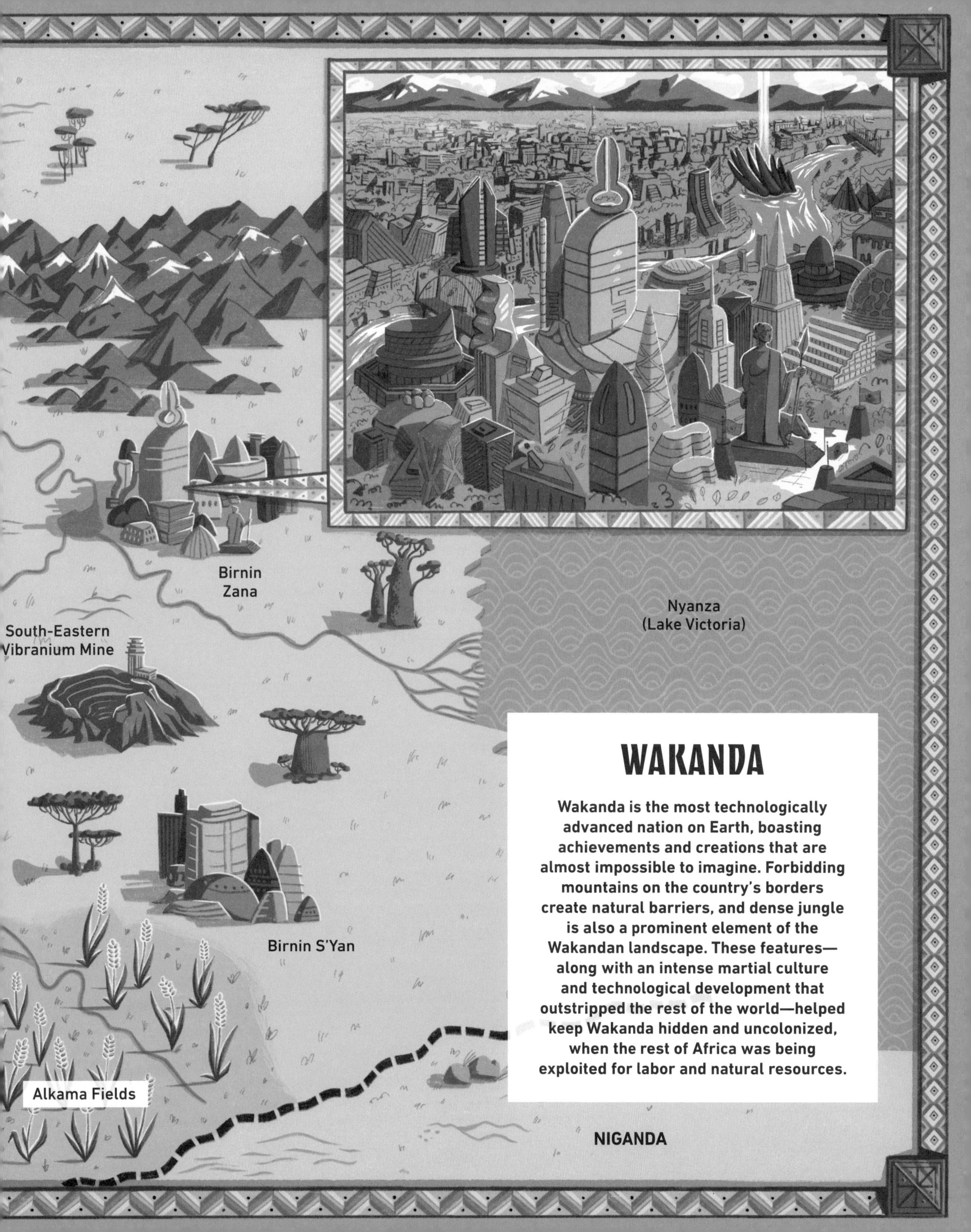

WAKANDA

Wakanda is the most technologically advanced nation on Earth, boasting achievements and creations that are almost impossible to imagine. Forbidding mountains on the country's borders create natural barriers, and dense jungle is also a prominent element of the Wakandan landscape. These features—along with an intense martial culture and technological development that outstripped the rest of the world—helped keep Wakanda hidden and uncolonized, when the rest of Africa was being exploited for labor and natural resources.

THE GREAT MOUND

The impact site and the remains of a giant meteor strike that contained vibranium are what make up the Great Mound. Also known as "Mena Ngai," the Great Mound is heavily guarded at all times with automated defenses and dedicated soldiers who keep watch over it around the clock.

Invaluable deposit
The Great Mound holds great spiritual significance in Wakandan culture, because of the way it has transformed the people's way of life.

PRECIOUS METAL

Ten thousand years ago, a massive meteor made of vibranium crashed onto the land that is now Wakanda. The Great Mound is the location of Earth's main source of vibranium. A single ounce of vibranium costs $10,000, making it one of the most valuable natural resources on the planet.

Pieces of the vibranium meteor splintered off as it entered Earth's atmosphere, scattering smaller deposits of vibranium all over Wakanda and other parts of Earth.

"OUR VIRTUALLY INEXHAUSTIBLE SUPPLY OF VIBRANIUM COMES FROM THAT SACRED MOUND WHICH HAS BORDERED THE LAND OF THE WAKANDAS SINCE THE DAWN OF TIME."

—T'Challa

THE DOOMWAR

One of the most cataclysmic events in modern-day Wakandan history was the Doomwar, which started when Doctor Doom attacked T'Challa and left him near death. The ruler of Latveria then invaded Wakanda and commandeered the nation's entire cache of the metal. King T'Challa used a mix of science and magic to render all vibranium all over the world inert. When the recent *Secret Wars* cosmic event rebooted the Multiverse, T'Challa's drastic measures were reversed and vibranium's natural properties were restored.

CHANGED LANDSCAPE

The animal life in the area around the Great Mound was profoundly affected by vibranium's unique properties. Dinosaurs still exist in Wakanda's shadowy hidden valleys, along with mutated humans and animals. Vibranium also affected the nation's plant life, with the most famous example being the heart-shaped herb that only grows in Wakanda.

RAW POWER

Prolonged exposure to raw, unprocessed vibranium ore can cause mutation, illness, or death. In the past, miners working in the Great Mound came down with vibranium sickness. Jakarra—half-brother to T'Challa and Shuri—purposely exposed himself to vibranium to transform himself into a powerful, monstrous form so he could fight Black Panther.

THE SACRED RESOURCE

Over the centuries, Wakandans used vibranium in important cultural practices. It has been used to create calming environments for childbirth, dampen noise during hunting ceremonies, and improve the efficiency of the nation's energy infrastructure. The desire to control vibranium has led to many conflicts in Wakanda and at its borders, either from native citizens looking to usurp power or outsiders who want the metal all to themselves.

WARRIOR FALLS

In central northern Wakanda is Warrior Falls, a cascading series of breathtaking waterfalls on a towering mountain cliffside. The site is one of the most beautiful places in Wakanda, however it has also beenn one of the most dangerous locations for King T'Challa.

Sacred grounds
Wakanda's fate has often depended on the ritual combat that takes place in this important location.

Although the nation's human inhabitants frequently fight in this area, Wakanda's animals have chosen to make a home here.

Black Panther hasn't won every battle waged at Warrior Falls, but he's always fought valiantly.

"LET THIS END WHERE IT BEGAN— AT WARRIOR FALLS."

—T'Challa

A GREAT FALL

When the expatriate Wakandan insurgent Erik Killmonger began an attempted coup d'etat at Warrior Falls, it was the start of one of the Black Panther's most important battles. Killmonger gained the upper hand and threw the Black Panther off the waterfall, seemingly to his death.

KANTU'S REVENGE

Killmonger suffered a resounding defeat in another battle at Warrior Falls. This time it wasn't King T'Challa who ended Killmonger's months-long vendetta against the throne. The decisive move was made by Kantu, a young boy whose father was killed as a result of Killmonger's campaign. Kantu rammed himself into Killmonger and knocked him off the falls into the rushing waters below.

A LONG BATTLE

Years later, Warrior Falls was the site of another fateful encounter between T'Challa and Killmonger. Killmonger's latest challenge to the throne saw T'Challa's rule threatened like never before, and the two men engaged in a cycle of ritual combat that took place over multiple days.

HEART-SHAPED HERB GARDENS

The heart-shaped herb grows in wild and remote locations across the Wakandan landscape. Braving the hazards of these locations to harvest the herb is a traditional part of the royal ascension ceremonies a person must perform to earn the title of Black Panther.

Super-special soil
Wakandan scientists believe that the heart-shaped herb only exists in Wakanda because of vibranium's impact on local ecosystems.

The herbalists who tend to the preparations of the heart-shaped herb use practices that have been passed down through multiple generations.

The ceremonies where Black Panthers are anointed with the heart-shaped herb are zealously guarded secrets within Wakandan society.

ADVERSE REACTIONS

Not everyone can safely ingest the heart-shaped herb. It can have disastrous side effects for those who aren't descended from Bashenga's royal bloodline, as Erik Killmonger learned the hard way. After a series of intricate political machinations and physical combat, Killmonger outmaneuvered King T'Challa and became the ruler of Wakanda. However, his body suffered a severe adverse reaction to the consumption of the heart-shaped herb, and Killmonger became comatose for an extended period of time.

A SECOND HERB

Another Wakandan herb, called Jufeiro, has allowed people who use it to place others under their mental control. A member of the Dora Milaje until she betrayed her station, the villain called Malice used it to undermine T'Challa's free will while he was captured. Malice also used Jufeiro to subvert members of Wakanda's Hatut Zeraze security forces into doing her bidding.

A REPLICA FORMULA

Once he woke from his coma, Killmonger created a synthetic version of the heart-shaped herb. He later offered it to New York City police officer Kevin "Kasper" Cole, who had been using a discarded Black Panther uniform to act outside the law. Killmonger's overture was an effort to recruit Officer Cole into his vendetta against T'Challa but the police officer wound up becoming an assistant of Black Panther instead.

THE DJALIA

Existing outside the bounds of time and space, the Djalia is the plane of ancestral memory, which holds the totality of Wakandan history. It can be accessed by scientific or mystical means, and visitors are guided by griot spirits who often resemble friends, loved ones, or other people they know in the real world.

What visitors see and experience in the Djalia is informed by their emotional and spiritual needs at the time of their visit.

Memory bank
The Djalia contains the memories of every Wakandan who ever lived, making it more populous than the physical representation of the realm.

Without a spirit guide, the risk of getting irrevocably lost in the Djalia is very high.

RECLAIMED HISTORY

T'Challa journeyed into deep space to search out the origins of vibranium, only to get pulled into a wormhole that displaced him into another galaxy. That galaxy was ruled by time-lost Wakandans who had created a conquering slaveholding empire. T'Challa became one of the enslaved, and later helped wage a long war of rebellion to free those in chains, whose memories had been taken from them. A pivotal act in that war was to empty the Djalia and restore the enslaved workers' personal histories. When they remembered who they were and where they came from, those laborers fought alongside T'Challa against the Imperial faction.

THE CABAL INVASION

During a time of multiversal crisis, a group of supervillains called the Cabal invaded Wakanda and left Princess Shuri in a state between life and death. Shuri was able to access the Djalia while she existed in this transitional state, walking through the living history of Wakanda and learning from a griot spirit that took the shape of her mother, Queen Ramonda.

THE ANCIENT FUTURE

T'Challa rescued his sister and brought her back into the land of the living. Shuri discovered that her time in the Djalia had endowed her with superhuman abilities drawn from the stories of history. The princess became known as Aja-Adanna, which means "ancient future" in Wakandan. She then used her powers to help end the People's Revolution, which was led by a plant-controlling magician named Tetu.

GENERAL NAKIA

General Nakia of the Maroons, who commanded an army of former nameless enslaved miners, was a key ally of T'Challa during the intergalactic war. She sacrificed herself in battle to buy time for other Maroon rebels to continue the fight for freedom. Though she appeared to have died, her soul found a new home in the emptied Djalia, which she now works to restore.

MUTE ZONES

The Mute Zones are villages in Wakanda where the inhabitants spurn advanced technology and choose to live according to historical traditions. This is done out of a distrust of surveillance and to honor the ways of their ancestors.

No data
Because they exist off the nation's informations systems grid, the exact populations of Wakanda's Mute Zones are difficult to determine.

Members of the Hatut Zeraze security force and other law enforcement entities often get a frosty reception in Mute Zones.

Drum circles and other older cultural folkways are found in abundance in Mute Zones.

Kimoyo bracelets are thrown away in Mute Zones to symbolize a rejection of modern, state-controlled technologies.

"WE DID THAT. HACKED THE SYSTEM TO LIVE IN FREEDOM."

—Okino, a Mute Zone teenager

LOW TECH

Some Mute Zones are so zealous with regard to secrecy that they don't even have names. Mute Zoners don't wear Kimoyo braclets like other Wakandans. They throw the multi-purpose Kimoyo tech-bracelets into the trees as a sign of defiance and people who wear them while visiting may have them stolen.

HIDE AND SEEK

Formed in the spirit of freedom, Mute Zone communities represent a quieter version of philosophical protest. Some of the people living in these areas are distrustful of Wakanda's technocratic hierarchy—which they see King T'Challa as a symbol of—while others wish to live in ways that are more in step with their ancestors. However, with their lack of surveillance, Mute Zones provide cover for those who have run afoul of the laws of the land, making them a tricky dilemma for Black Panther.

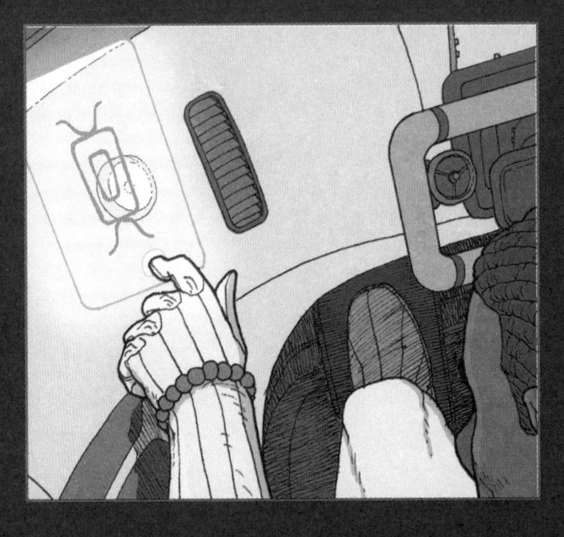

OFF THE GRID

In every Mute Zone, a group of teenagers hacks the infrastructure to set up private firewalls that erase the area from GPS, internet, and other telecommunications networks. Any vehicles or devices that rely on those networks are essentially rendered useless.

BIRNIN AZZARIA

Also known as the "Learned City," Birnin Azzaria is home to Wakanda's most vibrant academic institutions where Wakandans from all walks of life learn to fulfill their potential.

Noble namesake
This city was named after King Azzuri, the paternal grandfather of T'Challa, who oversaw a massive expansion of educational services during his reign.

The schools in Birnin Azzaria offer instruction in everything from agriculture to quantum physics.

If they meet academic qualifications, native Wakandans can attend the Learned City's colleges and universities free of charge.

EXTRACTION ACADEMY

At the Extraction Academy, students learn the disciplines of refining, shaping, and working with Wakanda's most precious resource, vibranium. Those disciplines combine into a field of study all unto itself and most Extraction Academy graduates finish their education ready to make great contributions to Wakandan society.

HEKIMA SHULE

Hekima Shule stands out from other Wakandan universities for its strong focus on philosophy and political thought. Its most noteworthy professor is Changamire, who was once a tutor for King T'Chaka's court until he fell out of favor for his anti-monarchist views. The insurgent shaman Tetu was a student of Changamire, but took a path of violence in trying to change Wakandan politics.

FINAL EXAM

Just as the confrontations between royal loyalists, renegade Dora Milaje, and the extremist People's movement were becoming more dire, King T'Challa appealed to the professor Changamire. A speech by Changamire roused a sense of brotherhood so strong it was able to interfere with Zenzi's psychic manipulation of the People's soldiers.

THE WAKANDAN SCHOOL FOR ALTERNATIVE STUDIES

Whether it's because of mutant genes, exposure to vibranium, or scientific experimentation, Wakandan citizens can sometimes exhibit superhuman powers. The Wakandan School for Alternative Studies exists to help Wakanadan superhumans understand and control their special abilities.

GIFTED AND TALENTED

Asha, a young woman with light manipulation powers, studied at the Wakandan School for Alternative Studies, along with energy absorber Block and enhanced fighter Bull.

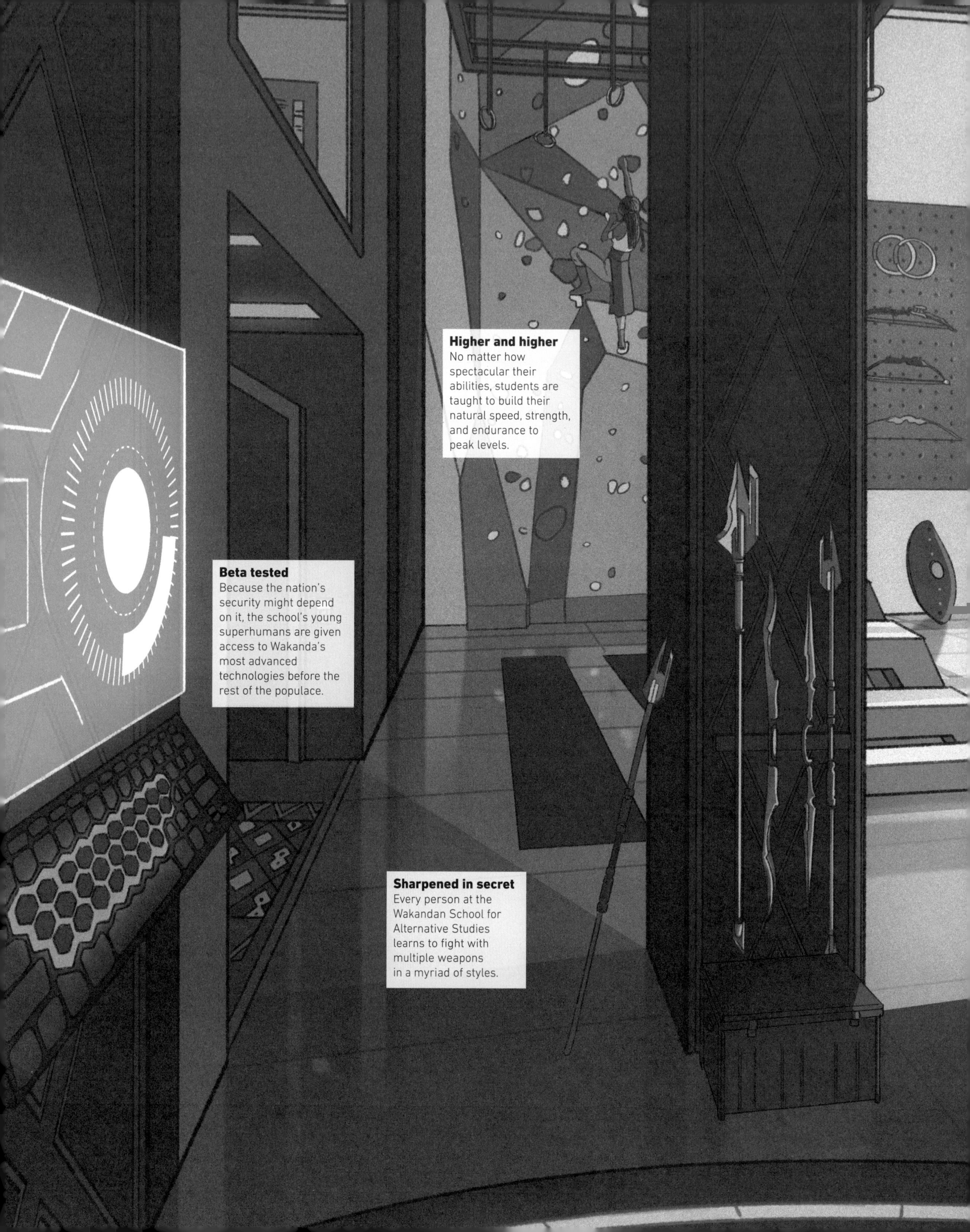

Higher and higher
No matter how spectacular their abilities, students are taught to build their natural speed, strength, and endurance to peak levels.
Beta tested
Because the nation's security might depend on it, the school's young superhumans are given access to Wakanda's most advanced technologies before the rest of the populace.
Sharpened in secret
Every person at the Wakandan School for Alternative Studies learns to fight with multiple weapons in a myriad of styles.

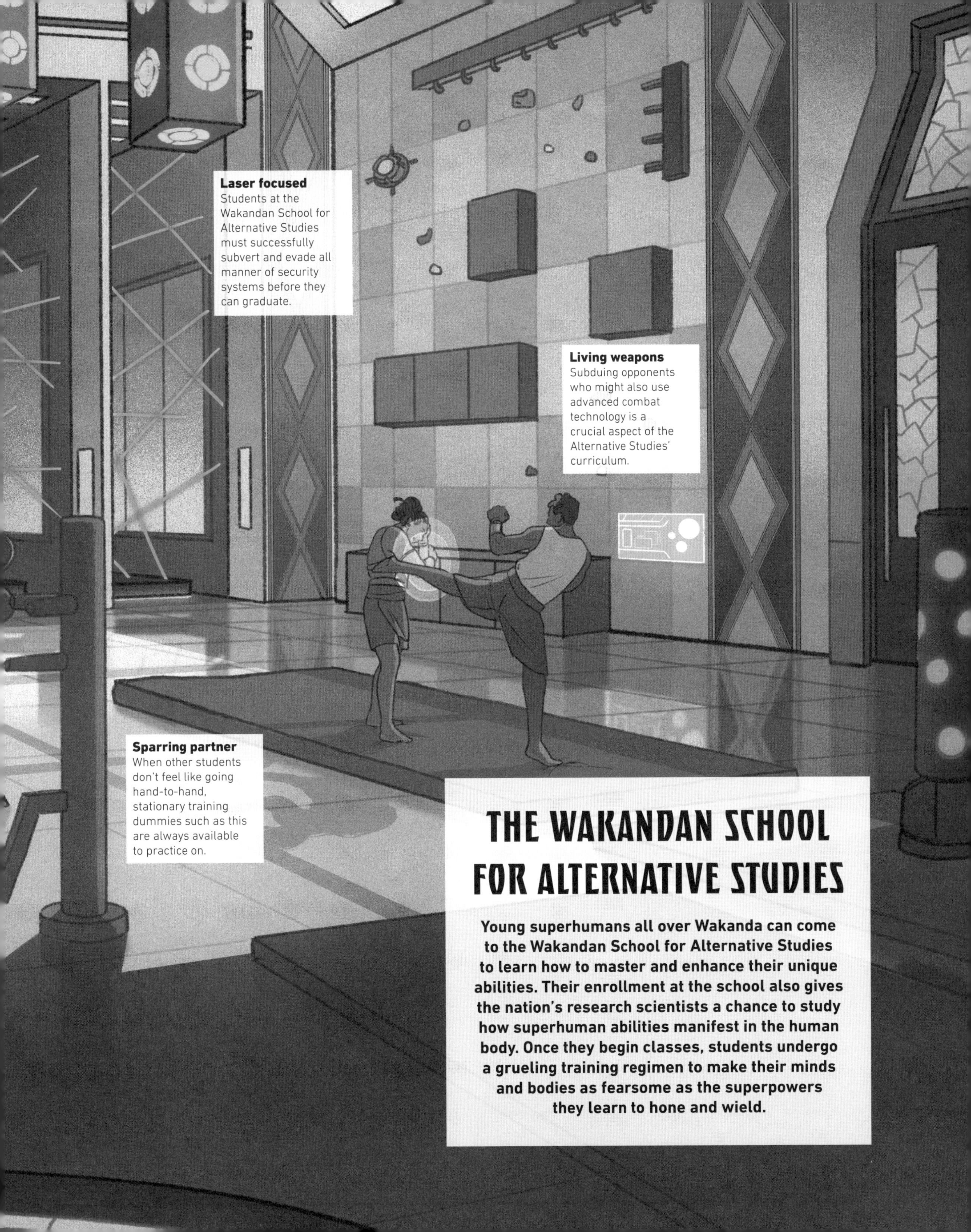

Laser focused
Students at the Wakandan School for Alternative Studies must successfully subvert and evade all manner of security systems before they can graduate.

Living weapons
Subduing opponents who might also use advanced combat technology is a crucial aspect of the Alternative Studies' curriculum.

Sparring partner
When other students don't feel like going hand-to-hand, stationary training dummies such as this are always available to practice on.

THE WAKANDAN SCHOOL FOR ALTERNATIVE STUDIES

Young superhumans all over Wakanda can come to the Wakandan School for Alternative Studies to learn how to master and enhance their unique abilities. Their enrollment at the school also gives the nation's research scientists a chance to study how superhuman abilities manifest in the human body. Once they begin classes, students undergo a grueling training regimen to make their minds and bodies as fearsome as the superpowers they learn to hone and wield.

N'JADAKA VILLAGE

Located in the Kinamasi region of Wakanda, N'Jadaka Village was the childhood home of Black Panther's fiercest adversary, Erik Killmonger (whose birth name is N'Jadaka). Killmonger may be seen as a villain by many, but those who inhabit his home village harbor a perverse pride in this connection.

Prodigal pride
Despite his murderous legacy, N'Jadaka Village doesn't deny that Killmonger was born in this community.

While T'Challa was tracking down Killmonger, he met people who suffered great loss because of the villain's terror campaigns beyond his village.

Even with all his skills and powers, the Black Panther has had to tread carefully whenever he's visited N'Jadaka Village.

FIERCELY LOYAL

It's not clear whether Killmonger seized control of the place where he was born or won the people's loyalty in some other way. But after his death and resurrection, the village was named after him and its residents wholly embraced Killmonger's political and military legacy.

OUT OF SYNC

Killmonger's legacy held so much sway that N'Jadaka Village separated itself almost completely from the rest of the country. The tiny village was transformed into a miniature metropolis, including a wholesale adoption of the outside world's ways that touched on everything from architecture to cuisine.

"I DISCARDED THAT NAME— IT'S NOW KILLMONGER."

—Erik Killmonger

HOME BASE

During his various campaigns to dethrone King T'Challa, Killmonger used his home village, which was dominated by an ominous watchtower, as headquarters for his soldiers and lieutenants. Despite its brutality and cruelty, Killmonger's opposition to King T'Challa won him followers across Wakanda.

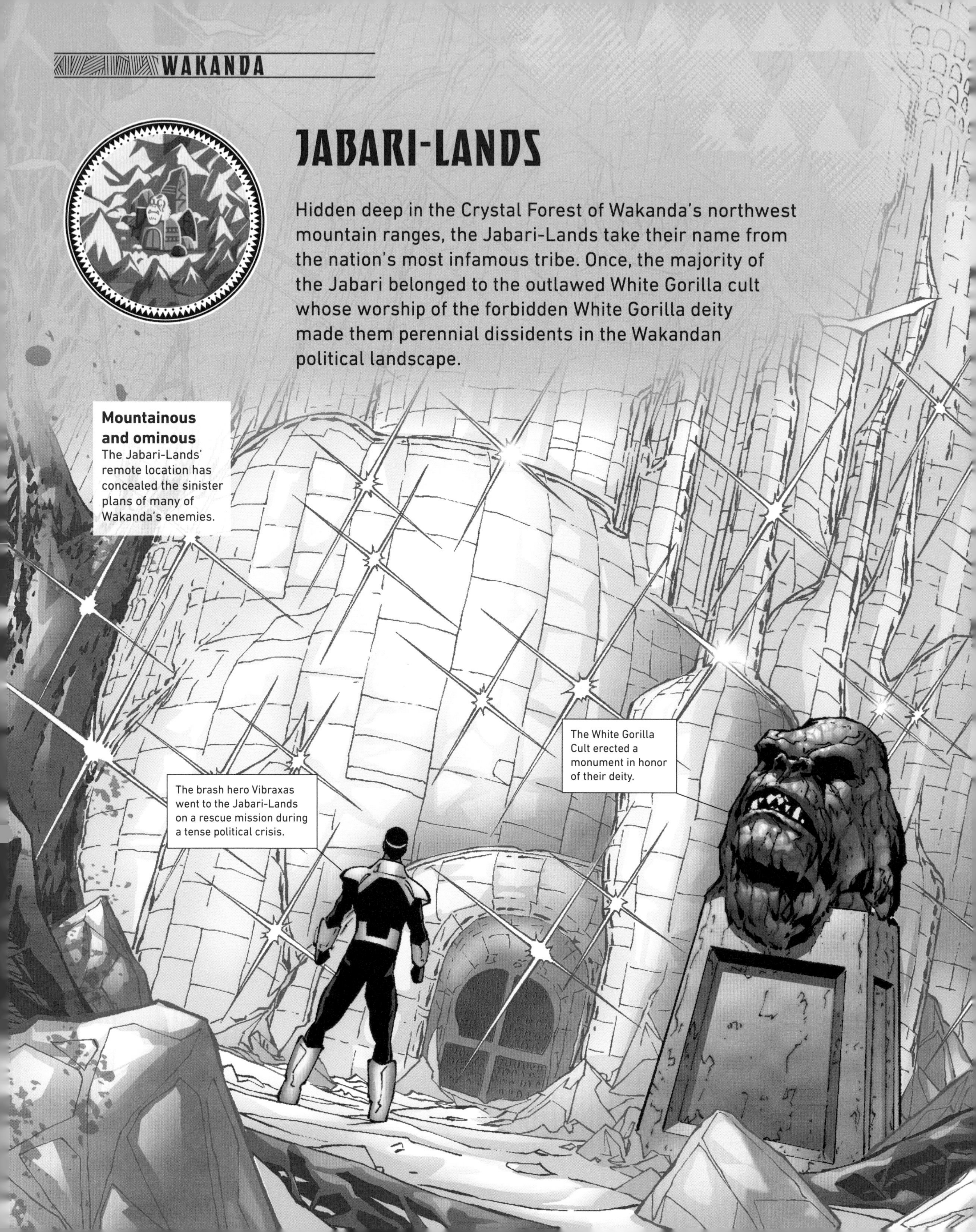

JABARI-LANDS

Hidden deep in the Crystal Forest of Wakanda's northwest mountain ranges, the Jabari-Lands take their name from the nation's most infamous tribe. Once, the majority of the Jabari belonged to the outlawed White Gorilla cult whose worship of the forbidden White Gorilla deity made them perennial dissidents in the Wakandan political landscape.

Mountainous and ominous
The Jabari-Lands' remote location has concealed the sinister plans of many of Wakanda's enemies.

The brash hero Vibraxas went to the Jabari-Lands on a rescue mission during a tense political crisis.

The White Gorilla Cult erected a monument in honor of their deity.

Harsh climates and difficult agricultural conditions hardened the Jabari people into some of the nation's fiercest warriors.

M'BAKU

When T'Challa became king of Wakanda and joined the Avengers, he installed his longtime friend M'Baku—a warrior from the Jabari tribe—as interim chieftain in his place. But once he came to the Royal Palace, M'Baku schemed to permanently steal the throne from Black Panther and adopted the supervillain identity of Man-Ape. The two men fought many times over the years, until M'Baku was slain in the Jabari-Lands by Morlun, a mystical predator who feeds on people who act as totems for otherworldly powers.

MANDLA

M'Baku's brother Mandla adopted his dead sibling's station and costume, presiding over a wave of corruption and abuse that festered in the Jabari-Lands while T'Challa was occupied with other matters. During the internal crisis fomented by the People's Revolution, Dora Milaje soldiers Ayo and Aneka delivered rough justice to Mandla and were joined by their sisters in establishing a new order in the remote mountains.

DORA MILAJE

For a time, the Dora Milaje rebelled against the Wakandan monarchy. Their break with the throne came when they learned that T'Challa was working with Namor the Sub-Mariner in secret after the Atlantean ruler's devastating tidal-wave attack on Birnin Zana. This rebellion brought the Dora Milaje into both physical and philosophical conflict with the king and his loyalists. But the end of the People's Revolution ushered in a moment of political and moral reckoning. Ayo and Aneka decided the Dora Milaje would still hold the Jabari-Lands as a territory unto itself, safeguarding it according to their own priorities while allying themselves with King T'Challa and the Wakandan throne as more equal partners.

ECHO CHAMBER

Hidden just beyond the outskirts of Birnin Zana, this noteworthy cave plays a part in the secret initiation rites of the Dora Milaje. The Echo Chamber's earthen cavity is shot through with vibranium, which generates several types of unusual phenomena.

Sonic strangeness
The Echo Chamber is yet another example of the bizarre phenomena that vibranium has created in Wakanda.

Dora Milaje initiates used high-security tablets to guide them to the Echo Chamber cave, and answered riddles that are part of their training process.

The eerie occurences that happen in the Echo Chamber deter local wildlife from taking refuge inside.

"WOW, THIS PLACE IS FULL OF VIBRANIUM! IT'S EVEN RESPONDING TO MY FOOTSTEPS. NOW I KNOW WHY THIS PLACE IS A DORA MILAJE SECRET..."

—Nakia

LOOKING FORWARD

Young initiates into the Dora Milaje have to enter the Echo Chamber and strike a drum that causes powerful vibrations within the cave. These vibrations reverberate through the initiate's mind and body, coalescing into a moment that gives them an unexpected glimpse of their future self.

SORORITY PLEDGE

The Echo Chamber's vibranium variant held a sentient consciousness that bonded tightly to the Dora Milaje because of their continuing interactions with it in the cave. When their discovery was brought to Professor Obinna Nwabueze—a gifted engineer who worked for King T'Chaka—he experimented with it and created the Mimic-27 weapon. The Dora Milaje decided it was too dangerous to use and hid it inside the Echo Chamber drum.

SECRET WEAPON

Nakia Shauku was a Dora Milaje who harbored an unhealthy obsession with King T'Challa. She eventually tried to kill a number of his loved ones and adopted the super villain identity Malice. In her quest for T'Challa's attention, she unleashed Mimic-27. The weapon created malevolent doppelgangers of Storm, Nightcrawler, and other heroes who tried to stop Malice.

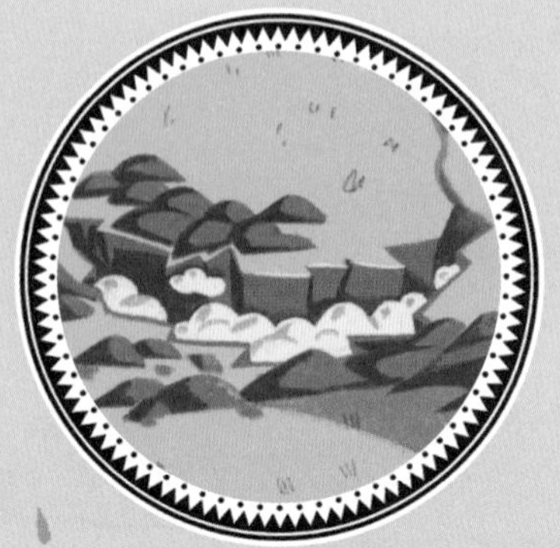

SERPENT VALLEY

Shrouded in fog and mist and home to living dinosaurs and other zoological anomalies, Serpent Valley stands as one of the most bizarre and foreboding places in Wakanda. It is possible that the meteor strike that created the Great Mound helped create an environment where dinosaurs exist.

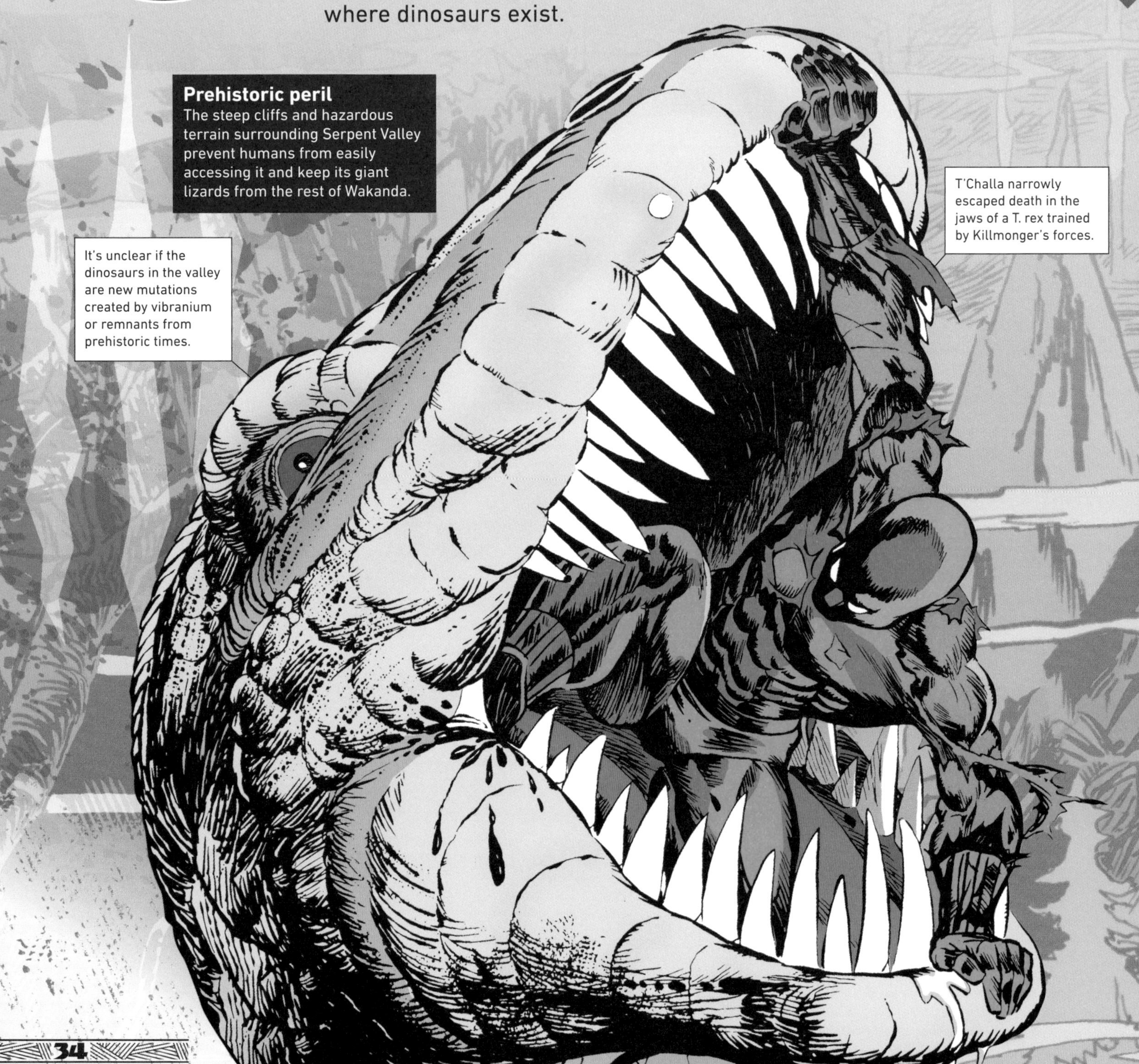

Prehistoric peril
The steep cliffs and hazardous terrain surrounding Serpent Valley prevent humans from easily accessing it and keep its giant lizards from the rest of Wakanda.

It's unclear if the dinosaurs in the valley are new mutations created by vibranium or remnants from prehistoric times.

T'Challa narrowly escaped death in the jaws of a T. rex trained by Killmonger's forces.

"THOSE SERPENTS... IF THEY EXIST... ARE OUR PURPOSE FOR ENTERING THE VALLEY."

—Killmonger

CAPTURED

During one of Killmonger's most audacious campaigns to take over Wakanda, he captured dinosaurs in Serpent Valley so he could later use them in his war against the Black Panther.

KILLMONGER'S CAVALRY

T'Challa's archenemy trained a Brachiosaurus and a Tyrannosaurus to carry soldiers into the heart of Wakanda and storm the Royal Palace.

PREYING ON THE PANTHER

Years after Killmonger's attempted coup, another Black Panther foe took inspiration from dinosaurs. Solomon Prey was the paramour of Tanzika, a woman who was exiled for attempting to kill T'Challa's girlfriend, Monica Lynne. Prey's plot involved genetically altering his own body to grow pterodactyl-like wings and claws. The experiments also masked him from T'Challa's super-senses.

ATTACKS FROM ABOVE

Prey also used Serpent Valley's giant lizards to attack Wakanda directly. The soldiers in his criminal operation sat atop Pteranodons that they steered via electrical controls grafted onto the beasts' bodies.

ALKAMA FIELDS

Located in southeast Wakanda, the Alkama Fields make up an important part of the country's agricultural ecosystem, providing many of the food staples that everyday citizens depend on. The region once belonged to the rival nation of Niganda, but was annexed by Wakanda during an infamously bloody conflict.

Bitter roots
Wakanda's most important agricultural province's history stretches back to a historical border battle with the rival nation of Niganda.

Niganda's defeat on these plains birthed a fiery hatred for Wakanda that burns to this day.

The battles fought on the Alkama Fields are the few times that Wakanda fought with expanisonist intent.

PERILOUS PRESENT

Wakandan insurgent sorcerer Tetu won over the people who lived in the Alkama Fields by using his ecological magic to end a drought. He then used the Alkama Fields as a hideout for the anti-monarchy movement called the People's Revolution.

OBODO AGHA

Reports of more mythological creatures prompted Black Panther and Storm to visit Obodo Agha, a village in the Alkama Fields. Their investigation found a nest of Anansi spider-beings that had been abducting local villagers.

STORMY WEATHER

After Tetu's revolution was quelled, the rains that he had summoned continued for weeks and flooded the Alkama Fields. King T'Challa was asked to investigate by local shamans in Birnin Kashin. He wound up battling a group of snake-men named the Simbi from a Wakandan myth, who emerged from a door of light in the Alkama forests.

HAUNTED BY HISTORY

After the incidents in Alkama, the true nature of the chaos was revealed. A villainous conspiracy had orchestrated the return of the Originators: the Anansi, snake-men, and other mystical species who lived on Wakandan land before the nation's founding. The Originators had been banished to another dimension by Wakanda's Orisha gods centuries ago.

BIRNIN ZANA

THE GOLDEN CITY

Home to the majestic Royal Palace, the Wakandan Constitutional Council, and some of the most advanced laboratories on the planet, Birnin Zana is the capital city of Wakanda. A long line of Black Panthers have ruled the country from this location, which is the place that T'Challa, Shuri, and the rest of the Wakandan royal family call home. Birnin Zana has survived attacks from foreign enemies and alien invaders, rebuilding itself to be stronger and more wondrous every time. Often referred to as The Golden City, Birnin Zana represents Wakandans' shining accomplishments and is the face that they are proud to show the rest of the world.

"THE GOLDEN CITY SHINES BECAUSE WE'VE BUILT A BETTER WORLD THAN THE ONE OUTSIDE THE WALLS."

—S'Yan

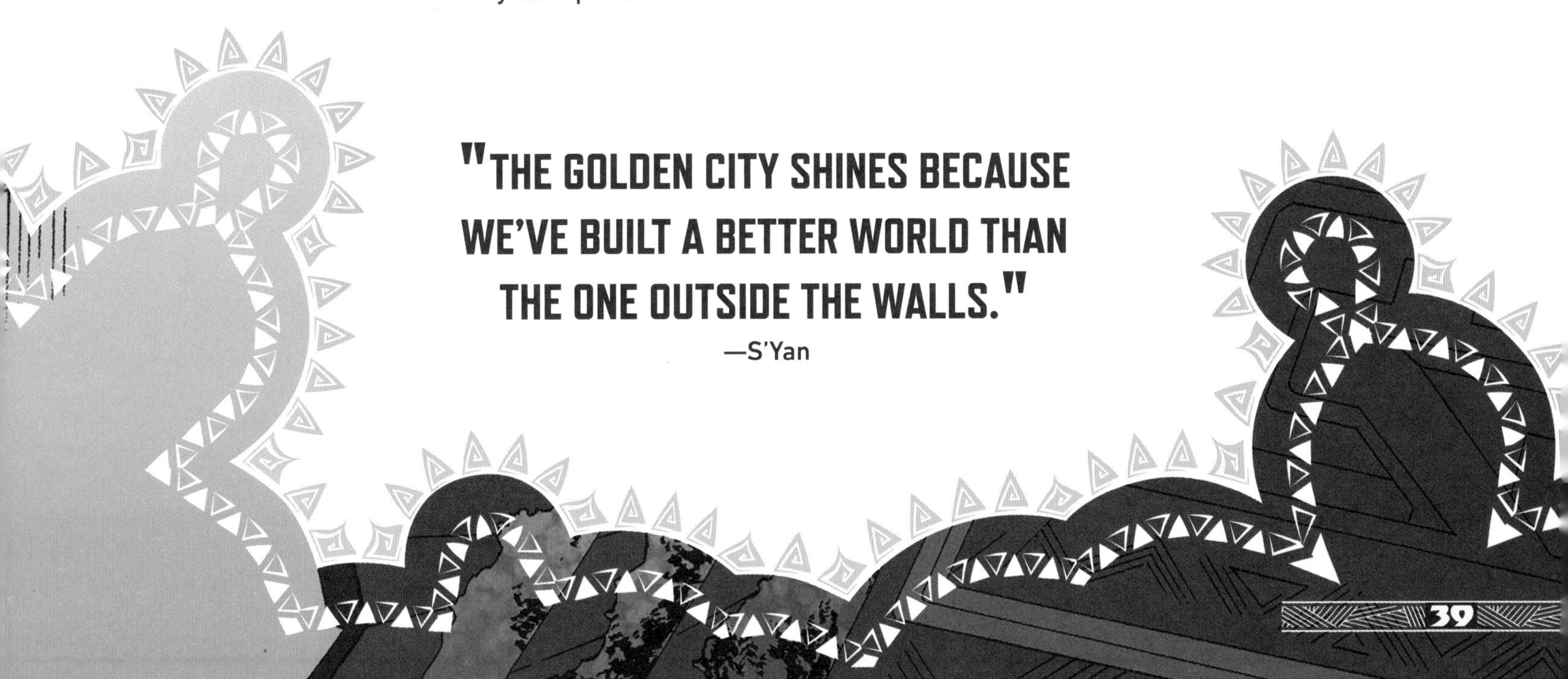

BIRNIN ZANA

Welcome to the Golden City! The capital city of Wakanda is the country's heart and soul. In a city of more than six million people, it is the nation's seat of royal, economic, judicial, and technological power. Birnin Zana is also the headquarters of Wakanda's famed secret police, the Hatut Zeraze, and the site of the Necropolis, the City of the Dead.

Necropolis
Upanga
Royal Palace
Nakia Memorial

THE TRIBAL COUNCIL CHAMBERS

Wakanda has been a monarchy for most of its history, but the monarchy has never operated in isolation. The nation contains tribes and factions with multiple priorities and needs, all demanding that their voices be heard. In years past, different meeting places have been used by representatives of these bodies for political purposes.

Righteous representation
Each tribal region in Wakanda sends delegates to the Council Chambers to put forth the area's political interests and agendas.

Cangza was advisor to King T'Chaka before T'Challa was born and served well into T'Challa's reign until he was murdered by Killmonger.

Tribal Council member Garouche opposed T'Challa's decision to introduce Wakanda to the world.

TAIFA NGAO

The Taifa Ngao, which translates to "Shield of the Nation", is one such organization comprised of elders who advise the throne. The advisors were a separate body and distinct from previous versions of the Tribal Council, who brought the concerns of their constituents to the throne so they might be addressed. Tribal representatives serve as a direct line of communication from the people to Wakanda's monarchs. Still, those who sat on the throne often followed their own plans, as when King T'Challa decided to publicly introduce Wakanda to the world.

THE WAKANDAN CONSTITUTIONAL COUNCIL

Wakanda's most recent political evolution has been the shift towards a constitutional monarchy, where power is shared more equally between council members and the throne. The change is a direct consequence of the People's Revolution led by Tetu and Zenzi. This insurgency helped T'Challa to realize he needed to get better at listening to the myriad voices that make up the Wakandan political body.

> "I WAS A DISCIPLE OF THE ELDER GODS WHEN YOUR ANCESTORS WERE BUT SUCKLINGS."
>
> —Zawavari

ZAWAVARI'S SANCTUMS

While Wakanda's advanced science and technology dominates the world's perception of the African nation, magic also thrives in the Unconquered Realm. Zawavari, a wily sorcerer who claims to have lived for centuries, is Wakanda's foremost expert on the occult arts. Zawavari has practiced his craft in multiple locations, including a deceptively simple hut away from the nation's urban centers. Some of these sanctums have been protected by magical guardians, like his home in the mystical area of Kummandla. The properties of this location enabled him to survive the death and rebirth of the Multiverse.

THE ROYAL PALACE

Located in the heart of Birnin Zana, the sprawling structure of the Royal Palace serves several important purposes. One such purpose is being the main home for generations of rulers and their families. It currently houses the living quarters of King T'Challa, Princess Shuri, and Queen Mother Ramonda.

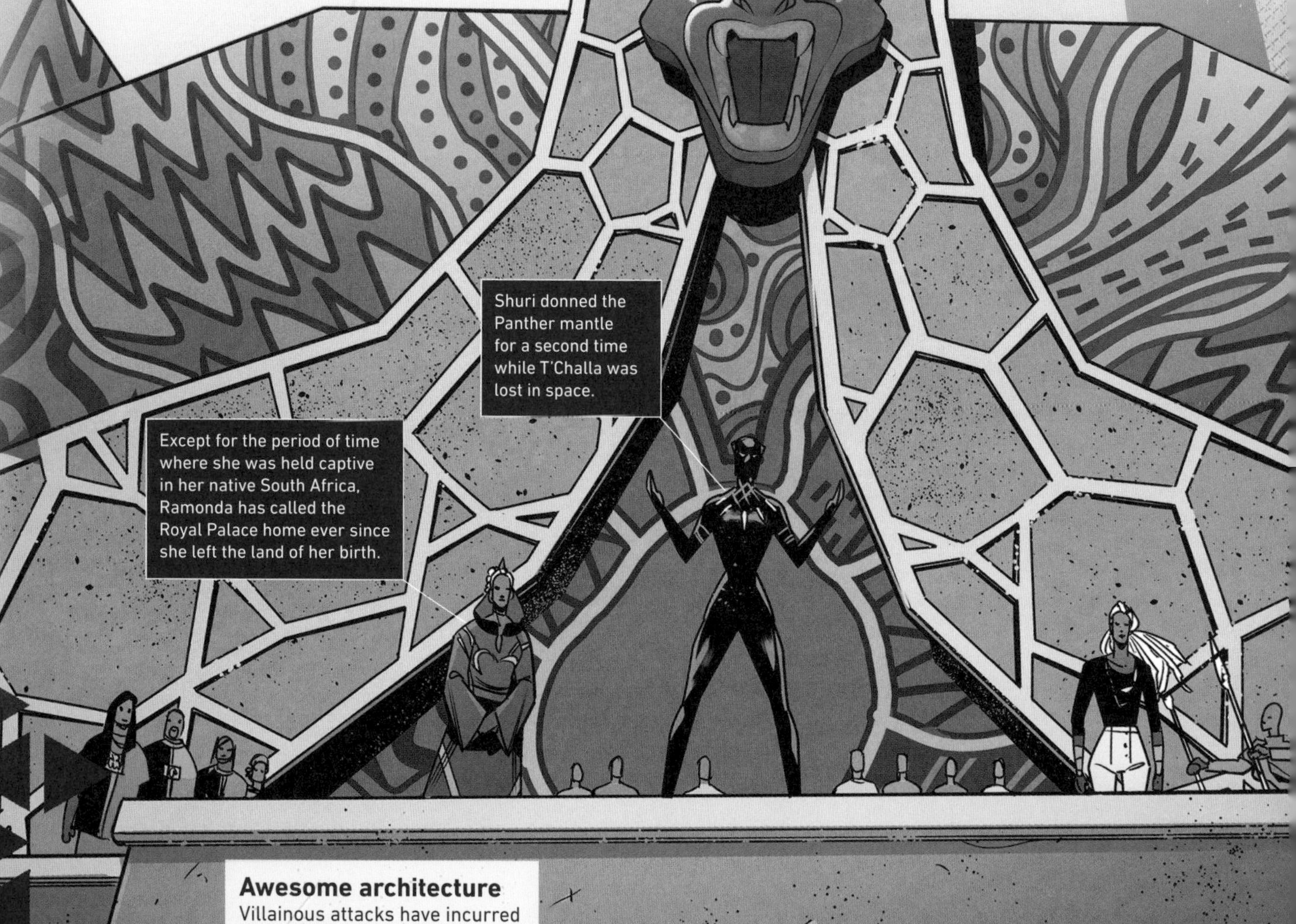

Shuri donned the Panther mantle for a second time while T'Challa was lost in space.

Except for the period of time where she was held captive in her native South Africa, Ramonda has called the Royal Palace home ever since she left the land of her birth.

Awesome architecture
Villainous attacks have incurred structural damage on the Royal Palace over the years, and it has been rebuilt numerous times with cutting-edge technology.

SECRET LABORATORIES

Both T'Challa and Shuri maintain laboratories in the palace. It also contains secret prototype vaults containing in-development research projects and experimental technologies that are only to be used in dire scenarios.

MILITARY WAR ROOMS

The Wakandan Royal Palace also contains chambers that serve as military war rooms, tribunal spaces, and temporary detention cells. Palace staff maintain a suite of vehicles in garages for rapid deployment into the field.

"IT'S JUST... REALLY... LIKE NOTHING I'VE EVER SEEN BEFORE."

—Ironheart

THE THRONE ROOM

The meeting chambers for the Constitutional Council and other governmental bodies are also within the Royal Palace. The throne room is also where Black Panther receives petitions from Wakandan citizens and greets diplomatic visitors.

SHURI'S LABS

Shuri's hi-tech rooms are located in the Royal Palace. These are innovative labs where Shuri dreams up the creations that help her pursue a mission of peace, stability, and justice.

Advanced inspirations
Sparked by the princess' genius-level intelligence, some of Wakanda's most innovative inventions begin in Shuri's labs.

Shuri can access all of Wakanda's surveillance systems from her labs to monitor events in any part of the country.

Holographic interfaces are just one of the tools that Shuri uses to parse through the terabytes of data needed to keep Wakanda safe.

FIRST FLIGHT

Shuri's time in the Djalia gave her multiple superhuman abilities, including the power of flight. That didn't stop her from using her lab to create a set of nanotech wings capable of getting her airborne. The wings' nano-materials deploy via mental or vocal command and can collapse into a cowrie shell on the princess' necklace.

"PERSONAL BIOMETRIC DATA, PORTABLE ENERGY STORAGE, AND THEIR PROJECTION CAPABILITY IS OFF THE CHAIN!"

—Ironheart

GRAND GARAGE

Despite having the power of flight and her wings, Shuri also invents other ways to get around on the ground. Her garage on the palace grounds houses multiple vehicles, but the foldable hovercraft she's used to travel to Mute Zones holds a special place in her collection.

TOOLS OF THE TRADE

Shuri first assumed the mantle of Black Panther after an ambush attack by Doctor Doom left her brother near death. While on a diplomatic mission in the United States, she was forced to battle a team of assassins. She and a team of espionage agents used cutting-edge weapons and gadgets to investigate anti-Wakandan forces. Shuri also crafted a formidable armored battle suit to fight King Namor of Atlantis.

WAKANDA DESIGN GROUP AND LABORATORIES

When products derived from Wakanda's cutting-edge engineering and research leave the nation's borders and go into the outside world, they do so via the Wakanda Design Group. The Design Group and its smaller entities located outside of Wakanda, are where Wakanda's most advanced creations are born.

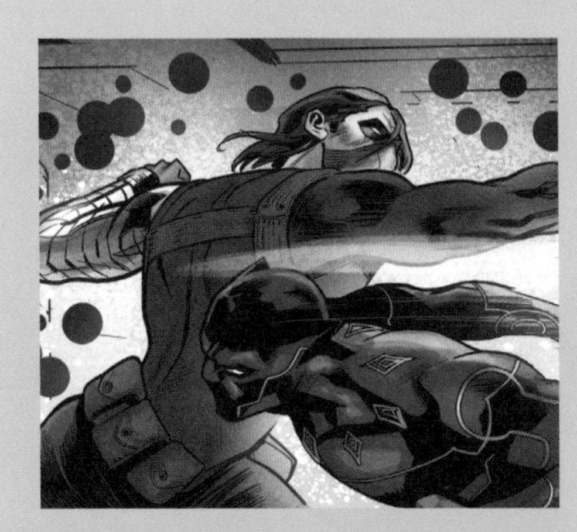

IDEA EXCHANGE

The Design Group was one of the first Wakandan organizations to have a persistent presence in the outside world. When diplomats from the United Nations were invited to visit Wakanda for the first time, one of their first stops was a tour of the Design Group facilities, led by King T'Challa himself. A rogue Russian spy agency called the Red Room learned of the visit and sent the Winter Soldier to infiltrate Wakanda and acquire intel on the nation's cutting-edge capabilities.

Brain trust
Many of the nation's most brilliant minds work at the Wakanda Design Group, making advances in countless fields of research.

T'Challa led a group of foreign diplomats on a tour of the Design Group before announcing Wakanda's existence to the rest of the world.

FLYING HIGH

Led in part by King T'Challa and Princess Shuri, the Wakanda Design Group serves as the primary exporter of vibranium-based technologies. One of the Design Group's best known creations is the first iteration of the Avengers Quinjet, which was designed by T'Challa and manufactured in partnership with Stark International.

RISKY BUSINESS

As a longstanding extension of Wakandan industry around the globe, the Wakanda Design Group has often been a target for those who want to illegally obtain vibranium or attack the Black Panther. When a secret intelligence conspiracy pitted Iron Man and Black Panther against each other, a majority ownership stake was part of the high-risk rivalry between the two heroes.

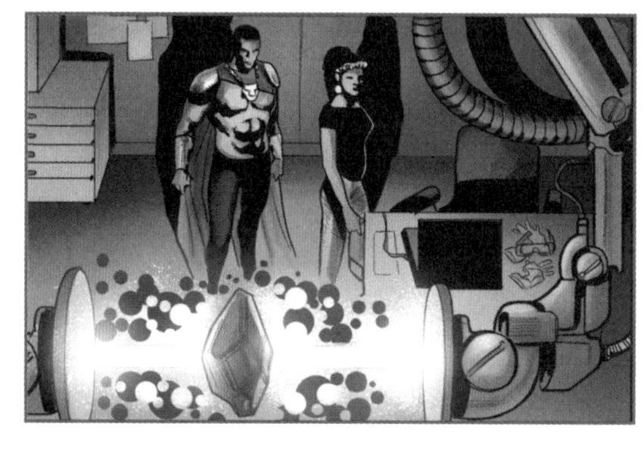

QUEEN N'YAMI'S LAB

Aside from the Wakanda Design Group headquarters, various unaffiliated and secret labs have existed in Wakanda over the years. Before she married King T'Chaka, T'Challa's birth mother N'Yami maintained a small private lab where she plumbed the secrets of vibranium. N'Yami later used a lab inside the Royal Palace after she accepted T'Chaka's marriage proposal. There, with a scientist friend named Takami from the Royal Scientific Development Division, she worked on infrastructure upgrades for the nation. N'Yami also designed weapons and armor that would be used by Black Panther and the elite Bashenga unit, a special squad that employed experimental technologies, when they thwarted an invasion attempt by evil terrorist organization Hydra.

BAD SCIENCE

Another lab facility in the southeast region was headed up by Takami, who worked with the Royal Scientific Development Division. Takami helped a repatriated Erik Killmonger conduct research on digitizing human memories. Unbeknownst to Takami, this technology was part of Killmonger's plan to defeat King T'Challa, and he died at the hands of the returned insurgent.

NECROPOLIS: CITY OF THE DEAD

Built up over many centuries, the Necropolis is a hidden city made up of the graves and memorial sites of fallen Panther kings. Because it serves as a living repository of Wakandan history, it is only accessible by Black Panther and the select few he chooses to admit.

Alive amongst the dead
T'Challa is the first living Black Panther to access the inner structures of the Necropolis.

Birnin Mutata is another name given to the Necropolis.

Accompanied by the Fantastic Four's leader Reed Richards, T'Challa met with a rare physical manifestation of the panther goddess Bast after being summoned by her in his dreams.

THANOS' CELL

An invasion by galactic conqueror Thanos devastated much of the capital city, and when it was all over Thanos was held captive in the Necropolis. Later, the Black Panther sought the counsel of his predecessors in the Necropolis. His ancestors told T'Challa that he needed to protect Wakanda above all else, even if it meant doing terrible deeds like destroying a whole planet.

THE WALL OF KNOWLEDGE

The Wall of Knowledge is the entrance to the city, which sits underneath the capital, Birnin Zana. The Necropolis' tombs pay tribute to Wakanda's previous kings and queens, and mausoleums contain artwork and sculpture portraying their most important battles and victories.

KING OF THE DEAD

During a time when Shuri ruled as the queen of Wakanda and T'Challa wasn't officially king, Wakandan goddess Bast anointed Black Panther as the King of the Dead. This title granted T'Challa the knowledge and experience of every monarch that preceded him, making his already impressive strategic prowess even more formidable.

ILLUMINATI BASE

T'Challa once used the Necropolis as a base of operations for the Illuminati, a controversial group of heroes, scientists, and mystics who were trying to save the world from crashing into Earths from alternate realities. These gatherings were held in secret. They caused massive tension between T'Challa and Shuri when she discovered that rival Atlantean ruler Namor—who had recently attacked Wakanda—was part of the Illuminati.

Clean air
Wakanda's focus on ecologically friendly technologies helps to keep Birnin Zana's air quality better than most other large cities.

BIRNIN ZANA MARKETPLACE

More than any other place in the country, Birnin Zana represents the beating heart of Wakanda. Whether they are engineers working with vibranium, herbalists healing via traditional methods, or farmers bringing food into the bustling city, citizens from all walks of life move through the nation's capital.

Techno chic
Whether it's modern spins on trendy styles or homages to traditional garb, most Wakandan fashions seen in the marketplace incorporate technological elements for aesthetic or practical reasons.

Inbuilt connectivity
Holographic projection capabilities in the marketplace's architecture let citizens publicly share images or videos. These can include anything from researching ancient folklore to advertising wares for sale.
Transport hub
Mag-lev trains and other forms of high-speed public transport woven throughout the kingdom make it easy for people from all over Wakanda to visit the capital city.

FORT HAHN

The inner workings of the Wakandan justice system are largely a mystery to the outside world but the nation has an effective court system, separate from the monarchy, where those accused of wrongdoing stand trial and verdicts are rendered by judges. Those convicted of crimes and those who dissent are locked away in Fort Hahn in the southeast of the city.

A DORA DETAINED

The Dora Milaje started acting independently of T'Challa upon learning that he had been meeting in secret with Namor after the Atlantean ruler flooded the Golden City during a battle between the Avengers and the X-Men. Aneka was one of the Dora delivering unsanctioned rough justice during this time of turmoil. She took the life of a brutal warlord who held women captive in the Jabari-Lands and was jailed for the killing for undermining the rule of law.

"WHEN THEY CONDEMNED YOU, DEAR HEART, THEY CONDEMNED ME."

—Ayo

Justice for all
The process of the Wakandan court system must contend with crimes that happen across the nation's many varied communities.

The Dora Milaje named Aneka was made to stand trial after killing a tribal leader who abused his power.

JAILBREAK!

Feeling that Aneka was unfairly sentenced, her lover Ayo—herself a captain in the Dora Milaje—broke the imprisoned warrior out of Fort Hahn. During the breakout, Ayo wore experimental Midnight Angel armor that high-ranking Dora Milaje deploy in extreme combat situations.

A GLASS CAGE

After T'Challa, Shuri, and their allies put down the People's Revolution, insurgent leader of the uprising, Tetu, was held in a special cell in Fort Hahn. A political professor named Changamire visited Tetu from time to time, but the superhuman's one-time mentor found a man who was unrepentant about the death and chaos he had caused. Tetu was later freed from imprisonment when a cadre of T'Challa's foes resurrected an evil deity called the Adversary in an attempt to conquer Wakanda.

The public trial of a Dora Milaje is such a rare occurrence that crowds of people assembled to witness.

UPANGA

Dora Milaje soldiers train at Upanga, a military institute that houses barracks and training facilities for the elite fighting force. Women come from all over the realm to train at this high-end facility.

While at Upanga, trainees learn to speak Hausa, the language the Dora Milaje use to communicate in secret.

Dora Milaje are expected to have expert knowledge of Wakanda's geography, so a significant portion of training happens away from Upanga.

Adored ones
Being chosen as a Dora Milaje initiate for one's region is one of the greatest honors that a young Wakandan woman can achieve.

"YOU ARE DORA MILAJE, CHAMPION OF OUR NATION, CELEBRATED IN FABLES AND SONGS."

—Ramonda

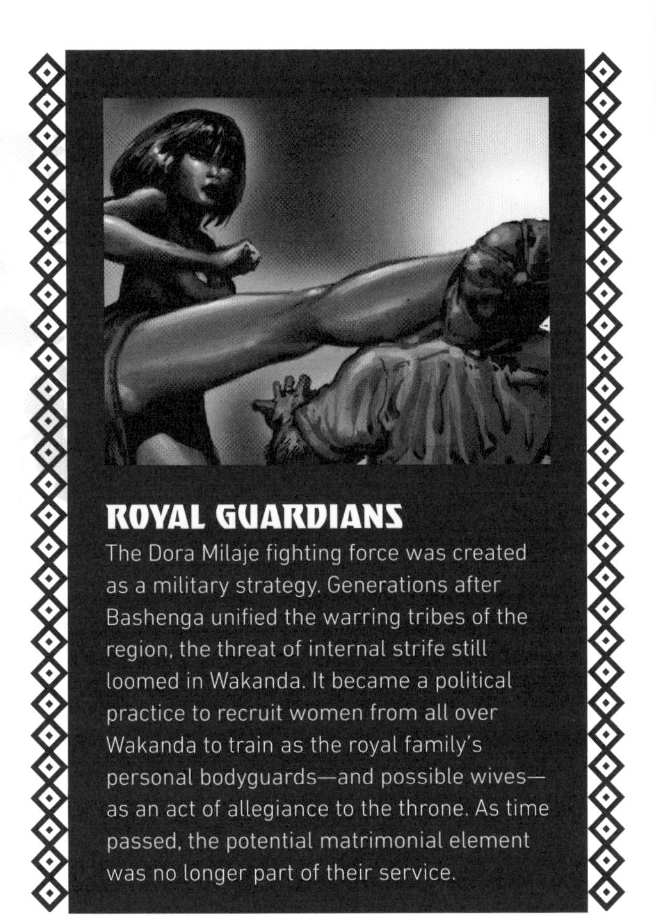

ROYAL GUARDIANS

The Dora Milaje fighting force was created as a military strategy. Generations after Bashenga unified the warring tribes of the region, the threat of internal strife still loomed in Wakanda. It became a political practice to recruit women from all over Wakanda to train as the royal family's personal bodyguards—and possible wives—as an act of allegiance to the throne. As time passed, the potential matrimonial element was no longer part of their service.

WARRIOR WOMEN

Women who sign up at the Upanga facility are called initiates, and they study Wakandan politics, history, and strategy in addition to hand-to-hand combat and weapons training. Initiates receive the distinctive head and face tattoos of the Dora Milaje as part of the Initiation Ceremony after they graduate.

MARCHING ORDERS

Mistress Zola runs the Upanga facility, overseeing the day-to-day operations, training protocols, and cadet discipline. The chain of command within the Dora Milaje has included some of Upanga's greatest graduates. Okoye, Director of the Agents of Wakanda, was previously a field commander of the Dora Milaje. She is a brilliant military strategist who also acts as one of King T'Challa's most trusted advisors. Prior to leading the splinter faction that rooted out corruption in the Jabari-Lands, Captain Aneka was involved in training recent classes of initiates.

BETRAYAL

When a young Dora named Folami started her training at Upanga, she was merely headstrong and resistant to her instructors. But she became more of a threat after allowing performance-enhancing nanites to be injected into her blood. Broken by the revelation that her father was part of the corruption in the Jabari village of Kagara, and by his subsequent death, she betrayed the Dora Milaje and sought revenge against the women who trained her.

NAKIA MEMORIAL

This statue commemorates the sacrifice of the Intergalactic Empire's General Nakia Cabral who helped repel the extraterrestrial invasion of Wakanda Prime. The towering tribute keeps watch over Wakanda in a public square in the nation's capital city of Birnin Zana.

Interstellar sacrifice
Nakia Cabral and T'Challa fought together to free the Intergalactic Empire's enslaved peoples.

ELITE ESPIONAGE

Nakia Cabral was raised in the House of Tafari amongst the elites on Planet Bast, enjoying a life of ease and privilege during Emperor N'Jadaka's reign. She grew up to become a spy and embarked on a mission to infiltrate the Maroon rebels who fought to free the imperium's enslaved peoples.

Used by both royalty and commoners, the spear serves as a symbol of Wakandans' readiness to protect the nation at all costs.

Nakia Cabral's statue holds a ring blade, a weapon favored by the Dora Milaje.

"ACROSS LIGHTYEARS AND MILLENNIA, SHE SAW A BEACON, A SIGN OF WHAT HAD BEEN AND WHAT YET MIGHT BE."

— T'Challa

CRISIS OF CONSCIENCE

The sins of the Wakandan space empire weighed heavy on Nakia's heart. It prompted her to defect in earnest and join the Maroons, a group of once enslaved beings who had rebelled against the Empire's discrimination and use of slave labor.

DUTIFUL DEATH

General Nakia helped turn the tide in a pivotal battle during the war between Wakanda Prime and the Intergalactic Empire, turning a massive spacecraft into a giant energy weapon that exploded as she fired on the Imperial armada. The friends and allies who fought beside her mourned her, not knowing that her spirit lives on in the Djalia.

TECHNO JUNGLE

The Techno Jungle's fusion of organic and manufactured elements is threaded through a network of sensors and data pipes that runs through Wakanda's jungles—hidden in trees and boulders—and underneath the nation's major population centers.

Integrated tech
The Techno Jungle is an expansive blend of technology and nature. It is perhaps the most astonishing feat of Wakandan engineering. It is woven through the nation's landscape in ways that are simultaneously hidden and out in the open.

The apparatus used in the Techno Jungle infrastructure undergoes constant upgrades.

COMMAND CENTER

The underground tunnels and catacombs that are part of the Techno Jungle house some of Wakanda's most dangerous weapons. After the conniving cleric Achebe schemed his way into a power-sharing agreement with Queen Mother Ramonda, he entered the Techno Jungle's tunnels, and used her access codes to launch giant panther robots called Prowlers, which were designed as doomsday weapons.

CAT CAVES

The Techno Jungle has served as a secret hideaway for Black Panther over the years, with secret access points in the Royal Palace and various pastoral locations. Its artificial terrain includes vast underground chambers with laboratories, security systems, and everything T'Challa needs to rule away from the throne. It also holds personal mementoes given to him by family and friends.

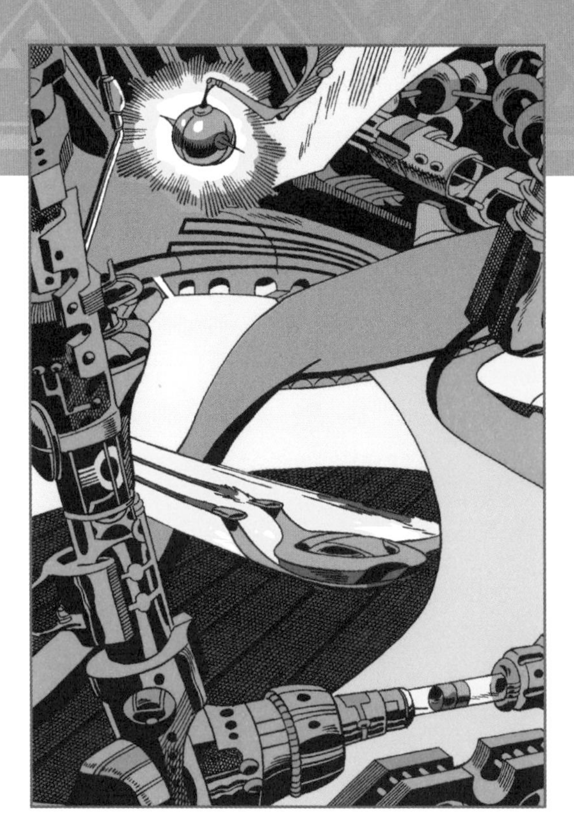

HIGH-TECH SECURITY

The Techno Jungle is a vital part of Wakanda's technological infrastructure. It contains security features that help keep unwanted outsiders from entering the realm. It also feeds military surveillance and telecommunications capabilities all over the country.

GOD VS. MACHINERY

Years ago, T'Challa used the hidden technology to do battle with an angry manifestation of the Panther God.

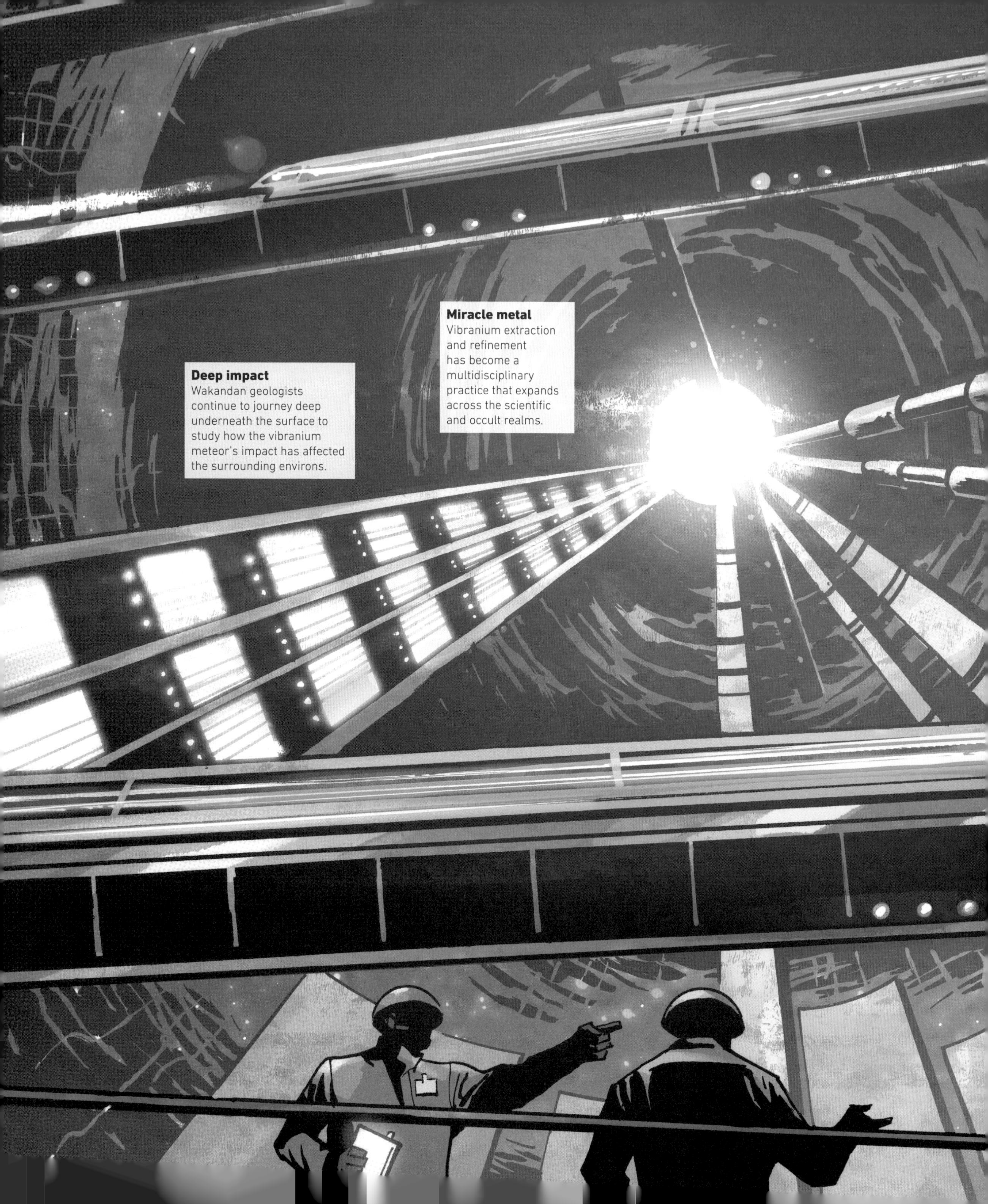

Deep impact
Wakandan geologists continue to journey deep underneath the surface to study how the vibranium meteor's impact has affected the surrounding environs.

Miracle metal
Vibranium extraction and refinement has become a multidisciplinary practice that expands across the scientific and occult realms.

VIBRANIUM MINES

The mining operations that extract vibranium rank amongst the most important of Wakanda's logistical infrastructure. The tunnels honeycombed through the Great Mound are connected by high-security transport platforms criss-crossing over miles-deep shaftways. To the untrained trespasser, the realm's various dig sites hold danger and wonder in varying amounts.

Smart networks
A mix of human and artificial intelligences monitor and control the railways that ferry workers, equipment, and ore at mining locations.

RESURRECTION ALTAR

Powered by the remains of a burned-out star, the Resurrection Altar acts as a focal point for supernatural energies which can be used to bring the dead back to life. Black Panther's archnemesis Erik Killmonger has made frequent use of the altar in his schemes to unseat the king of Wakanda.

Twinkle twinkle
It's believed that the altar's energies emanate from the remains of a star.

Sombre, another ally of Killmonger, also received strange powers from Resurrection Altar.

Beings like King Cadaver, already transformed by the altar, could be made stronger by repeated exposures.

ELDRITCH EVIL

Erik Killmonger empowered his lieutenant King Cadaver with the unique energies of the Resurrection Altar, granting Cadaver telepathic powers and enhanced strength.

ALTAR OF ANGER

Black Panther's archenemy also used Resurrection Altar to create more Death Regiments during another coup attempt. T'Challa enlisted the help of occult hero Doctor Voodoo to thwart Killmonger's plans.

UNDEAD ARMIES

Under Killmonger's orders, King Cadaver also used those same energies to create Death Regiments—armies of undead soldiers—to wage war against the Black Panther. Those regiments were commanded by Cadaver's underling Baron Macabre, whose corpse-like body could fire blasts of lethal energy.

LIVE EVIL

Killmonger himself has been returned from death several times at the Resurrection Altar. One of those instances saw his loyal followers performing a ritual where their own deaths allowed Killmonger's consciousness to take up residence in another man's body.

"CADAVER HAS BEEN RESURRECTED. HIS FORMER LIFE HAS CEASED TO EXIST."

—Killmonger

BEYOND THE BORDERS

Whether Wakanda has been hidden or publicly known, it has always had to reckon with the outside world. Threats to the Unconquered Realm come from all corners of the Earth, and the Black Panther and his allies have often had to fight their battles in foreign lands or engage in geopolitical diplomacy to preserve peace.

"TODAY, I AM TAKING THE FIRST STEPS TOWARD ENDING THAT ISOLATION. THE WORLD WILL SEE WAKANDA AND KNOW OUR STRENGTH."

—T'Challa

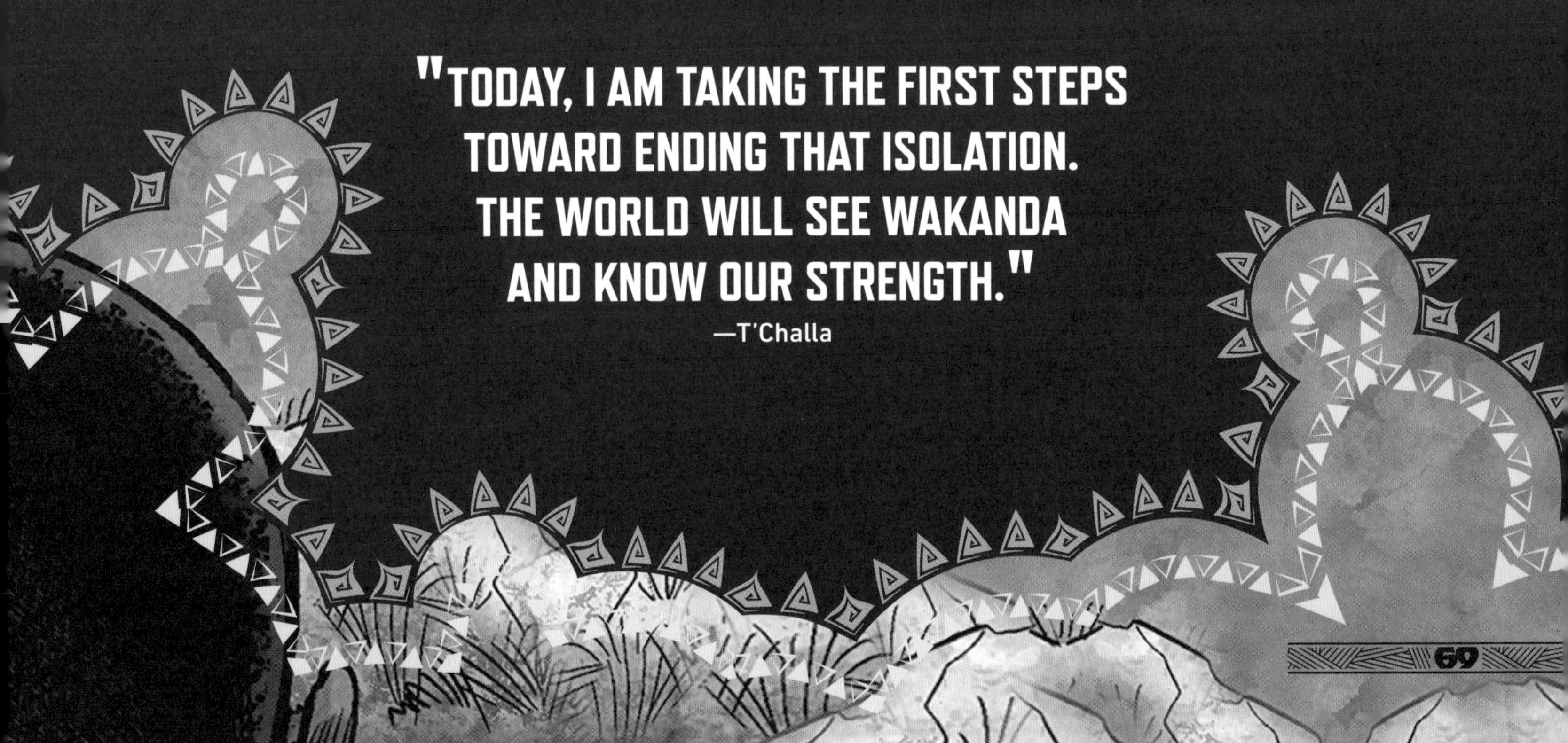

NIGANDA

A hostile nation bordering Wakanda to the southeast, Niganda's enmity toward the more prosperous kingdom of Wakanda has been the cause of much strife. Niganda has partnered with many enemies of Wakanda and even served as a base of operations for Erik Killmonger.

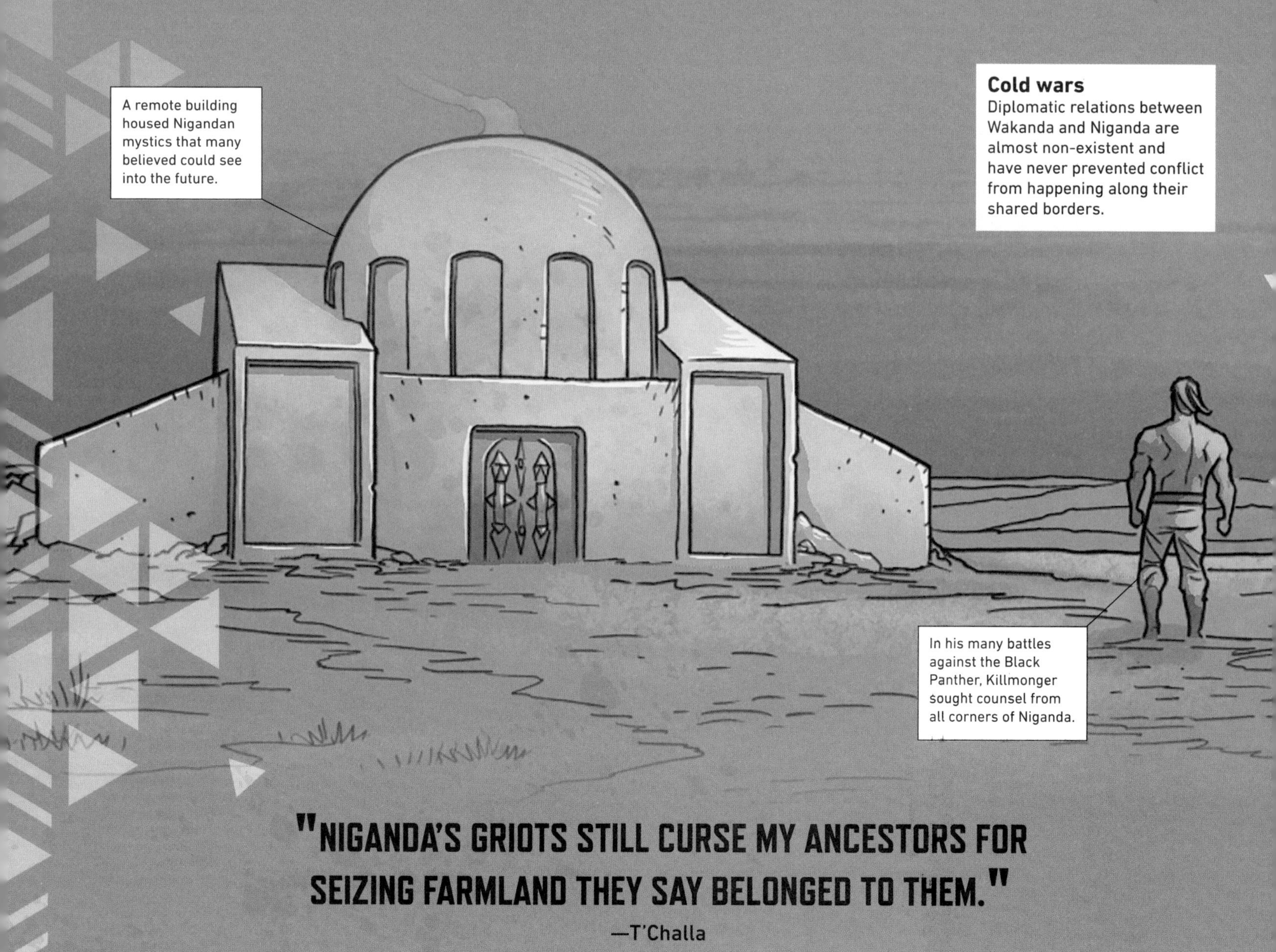

A remote building housed Nigandan mystics that many believed could see into the future.

Cold wars
Diplomatic relations between Wakanda and Niganda are almost non-existent and have never prevented conflict from happening along their shared borders.

In his many battles against the Black Panther, Killmonger sought counsel from all corners of Niganda.

"NIGANDA'S GRIOTS STILL CURSE MY ANCESTORS FOR SEIZING FARMLAND THEY SAY BELONGED TO THEM."

—T'Challa

ANGRY NEIGHBOR

Long ago, the fertile Alkama Fields were the domain of Niganda until they were taken by Wakanda in a bloody conflict. This loss created a deep-seated resentment that has only grown and festered over the centuries. Because of its proximity to the Unconquered Realm and its hostile stance towards Wakanda, Niganda has often offered support to the nation's foes.

A MALICIOUS STRATEGY

Erik Killmonger is among those who have used northwestern Niganda as a staging area for campaigns attempting to put an end to Wakandan sovereignty. While based in Niganda, Killmonger conducted a reign of terror that included mass killings and unethical experiments. The superhuman powers of Zenzi—the psychic manipulator who aided Tetu in the People's Revolution—were a direct result of Killmonger's presence in Niganda.

SINISTER ABDUCTIONS

Soon after T'Challa became king, he began investigating a string of disappearances of Wakandan citizens stretching back to the time before his reign. The trail led to an early confrontation with Namor of Atlantis, but the two rulers found that the true culprit was General Zoruun of Niganda. The military leader was working with support from the apartheid state of Azania and the Atlantean traitor Meranno to try and steal secrets from the kidnapped Wakandans.

KILLMONGER'S TOMB

After Killmonger's death, he was interred in Niganda and guarded by loyalist soldiers. His remains were exhumed by Tetu and Zenzi and brought to the Resurrection Altar so that the extremist villains could implant the fused consciousness of Emperor N'Jadaka and an alien symbiote into his body.

AZANIA

Bordering Wakanda to the southwest, Azania is a country that has long adhered to a racist governmental rule that kept its Black population as second-class citizens.

Colonized capital
The epicenter of Azania's political machinery is the city of Fischerstadt, whose name signals back to the settlers who exploited the land.

The Azanian government turned its military on innocent citizens in retaliation for anti-apartheid protests.

Azania's villages do not have the technological protections that their neighbors in Wakanda do.

APARTHEID ANTAGONISM

After generations of subjugation and suppressed rebellion, Azania's Black citizens found hope when it seemed like the Black Panther became directly involved in the struggle for their freedom. However, in reality, King T'Challa favored a diplomatic stand against the institutional injustice that kept the Black Azanians down.

AVATAR OF ANGER

Displeased with this choice, the spiritual manifestation of the Black Panther's power left T'Challa and embedded itself in an imprisoned Azanian man. Transformed into a vicious werecat, this avatar began killing white Azanians in retaliation for their brutal oppression.

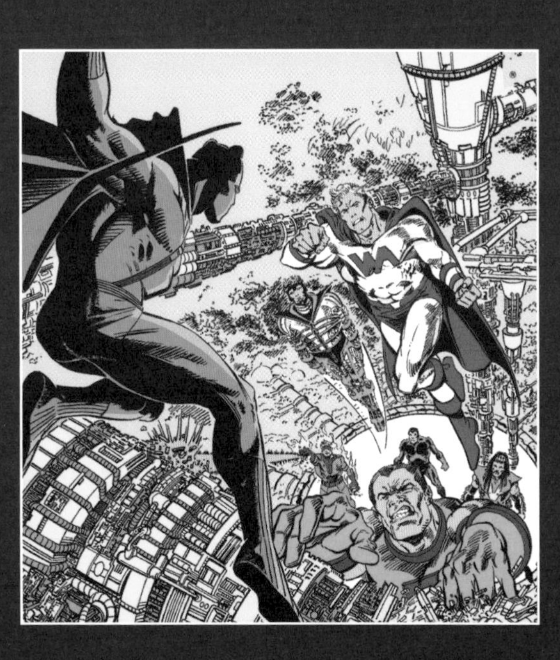

ENHANCED ENEMIES

The white Azanian government believed that King T'Challa was aiding the anti-apartheid rebels and sent a team of superhumans called the Supremacists to attack him in Wakanda. The Supremacists' goal was to take T'Challa into custody but, when he eluded capture, they began a campaign of terror in Wakanda. King T'Challa ended their rampage by turning their abilities against them.

NUCLEAR STRIKE

After the Supremacists' defeat, General Moorbecx of Azania escalated matters further by authorizing a nuclear strike on the heart of Wakanda. T'Challa was captured when infiltrating the missile base but was later freed by the Panther Spirit's new incarnation. He then fought the Azanian military and stopped the missile from striking Wakanda.

WAKANDAN EMBASSY

Wakanda's diplomatic mission, located in New York City, is the nation's main site of political interface in the outside world.

Home away from home
A plaque with the words "Awazili n'gyato imo sabolari"—"To embrace the global village" in English—adorns the outside of the Wakandan Embassy in New York.

The United Nations banner and Wakandan flag fly side-by-side to symbolize international cooperation.

In times of political tension, armed guards are stationed outside the embassy.

ENGAGEMENT ANNOUNCEMENTS

The Wakandan Embassy has served as the site for important personal and political announcements concerning Wakanda and the lives of its royal family. When it came time to tell the world that King T'Challa and Storm were engaged to be married, it was done via a press conference held at the embassy.

"WAKANDA'S FUTURE RESTS IN THE ABILITY TO CREATE TRUST BEYOND OUR BORDERS."

—T'Challa

INTERNATIONAL RELATIONS

Enemies of King T'Challa have turned public opinion against him in the past. When these manipulations—or sometimes the actual actions of the Black Panther or Wakanda—cause anger in the outside world, the Wakandan embassy has been a site of protest.

Masked legacy
The larger-than-life renditions of Black Panther masks remind visitors of the long lineage of those who have protected Wakanda over the centuries.

INSIDE THE WAKANDAN EMBASSY

For the vast majority of the outside world, the Wakandan Embassy is the closest they will ever get to the Unconquered Realm. Like the enigmatic nation it serves as an outpost for, the modest structure contains secrets that most visitors will never encounter. Despite Wakanda's isolationist bent, the soul of the nation can still be felt via the artifacts from Wakandan history and advanced technologies that the embassy proudly displays.

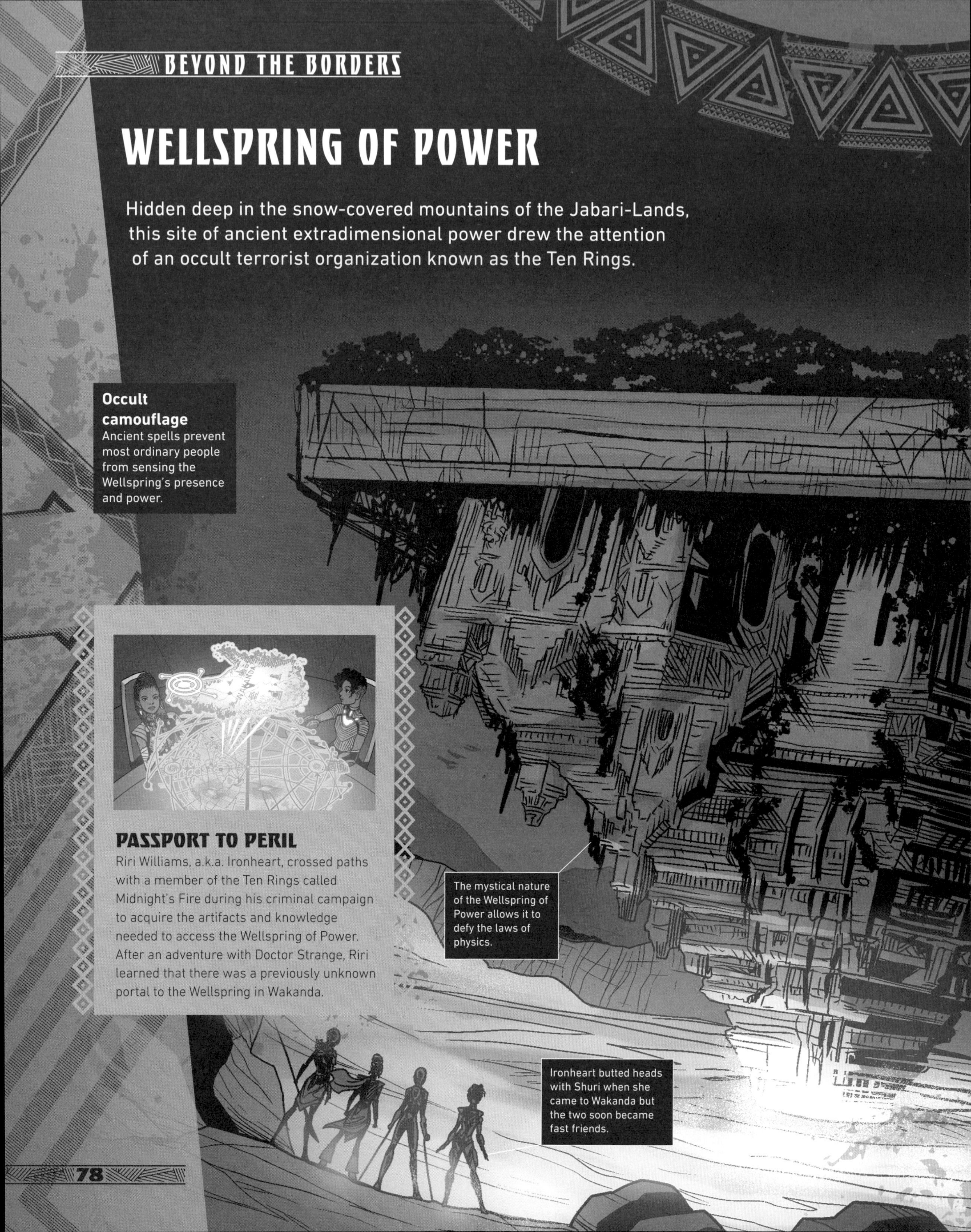

WELLSPRING OF POWER

Hidden deep in the snow-covered mountains of the Jabari-Lands, this site of ancient extradimensional power drew the attention of an occult terrorist organization known as the Ten Rings.

Occult camouflage
Ancient spells prevent most ordinary people from sensing the Wellspring's presence and power.

PASSPORT TO PERIL

Riri Williams, a.k.a. Ironheart, crossed paths with a member of the Ten Rings called Midnight's Fire during his criminal campaign to acquire the artifacts and knowledge needed to access the Wellspring of Power. After an adventure with Doctor Strange, Riri learned that there was a previously unknown portal to the Wellspring in Wakanda.

The mystical nature of the Wellspring of Power allows it to defy the laws of physics.

Ironheart butted heads with Shuri when she came to Wakanda but the two soon became fast friends.

PORTALS ABOUNDING

Midnight's Fire learned of the Wellspring while growing up with his grandmother Tai, who had long schemed to tap into its cosmic energies. During an attempt to recruit Ironheart to his cause, he revealed that other portals to the Wellspring on Earth had been sealed.

"THE WELLSPRING IS A PATHWAY THROUGH THE FOLDS OF OUR VERY UNIVERSE."
—Silhouette

DARK ADVERSARIES

Ironheart's quest led to a prickly team-up with Shuri, and the two heroes found themselves fighting shadow creatures erupting from the ground during an unnatural earthquake in Birnin Zana.

MOUNTAINS OF MADNESS

Shuri and Ironheart were joined by fellow hero Silhouette, the sister of Midnight's Fire. Silhouette's continuing mission to foil her brother's plots brought her to Wakanda, and the three women journeyed to the Jabari-Lands together. Once there, they were joined by General Okoye of the Dora Milaje and fought Jabari tribesmen who had been taken over by the same dark energy that had threatened Birnin Zana.

VIBRANIUM

KINETIC POWER

Vibranium is processed and deployed for many scientific and military uses. Its most common application is to absorb and redirect kinetic energy, as often seen in King T'Challa's Black Panther suit. Vibranium has also been shown to capture or deflect light to make objects invisible, as well as to disintegrate matter by disrupting the molecular energy that binds it together.

INVADING INTERLOPERS

Opportunists from the outside world have long sought to illegally acquire vibranium. The most infamous attempt happened when scientist Ulysses Klaw came to Wakanda to plunder the nation's sacred metal. In the battle that followed, T'Challa's father King T'Chaka died protecting Wakanda's most precious resource.

ANTI-METAL

Anti-metal is another variant of vibranium, and is commonly found in the Antarctic hidden jungles known as the Savage Land. Anti-metal doesn't affect energy like its Wakandan counterpart, but it does possess the ability to break down other forms of metal. Reverbium is a synthetic version of Wakandan vibranium, with all the same abilities in a more unstable form.

VOLATILE

Depending on factors like mass and engineering processes, there is an upper limit to the amount of energy that vibranium can absorb. At first, the captured energy strengthens the molecular bonds of vibranium, making it more durable. Past a certain point, vibranium's ability to absorb energy reaches maximum capacity, often resulting in an explosive event that destroys the metal itself.

SENTIENT VIBRANIUM

The Avengers' robotic archenemy Ultron once called vibranium "the most versatile substance on the planet." Wakandan scientists have found that, in certain rare conditions, the super-metal has even harbored its own rudimentary thought processes. This ultra-rare variant is called "sentient vibranium."

SOUTHEAST VIBRANIUM MINES

Once a dangerous deposit of the extraterrestrial super-metal, these mines can now be worked safely thanks to Wakanda's most brilliant mind.

CORAL CRISIS

This particular sector of the Wakandan mining infrastructure harbors a unique fungus called vibe coral. Mutated after centuries of exposure to vibranium, vibe coral can induce hallucinatory visions in those exposed to it. A special anti-fungal medicine developed by Princess Shuri can counter vibe coral's adverse side effects.

BUG HUNT

The southeast mines were one of the sites endangered by the Space Lubber, an insectoid alien that Shuri encountered in space while looking for her missing brother. Shuri was aided by Storm and a friend named Muti, who used his mutant powers of techno-kinesis in the Djalia while Shuri established a connection with the Space Lubber to find a peaceful resolution to its problems.

INTERSTELLAR EXPANSIONS

Black Panther's adventures have often taken him beyond Earth's orbit, either as a member of formidable Super Hero teams or on far-flung journeys where his memory and the Wakandan cultural identity seemed irrevocably lost. After an extraterrestrial mission to find the origins of vibranium went awry, T'Challa found himself in a sector of space called the Intergalactic Empire of Wakanda.

"ACROSS THE VASTNESS OF SPACE, I SAW THE VERY NAME OF WAKANDA EXPAND."

—Bast

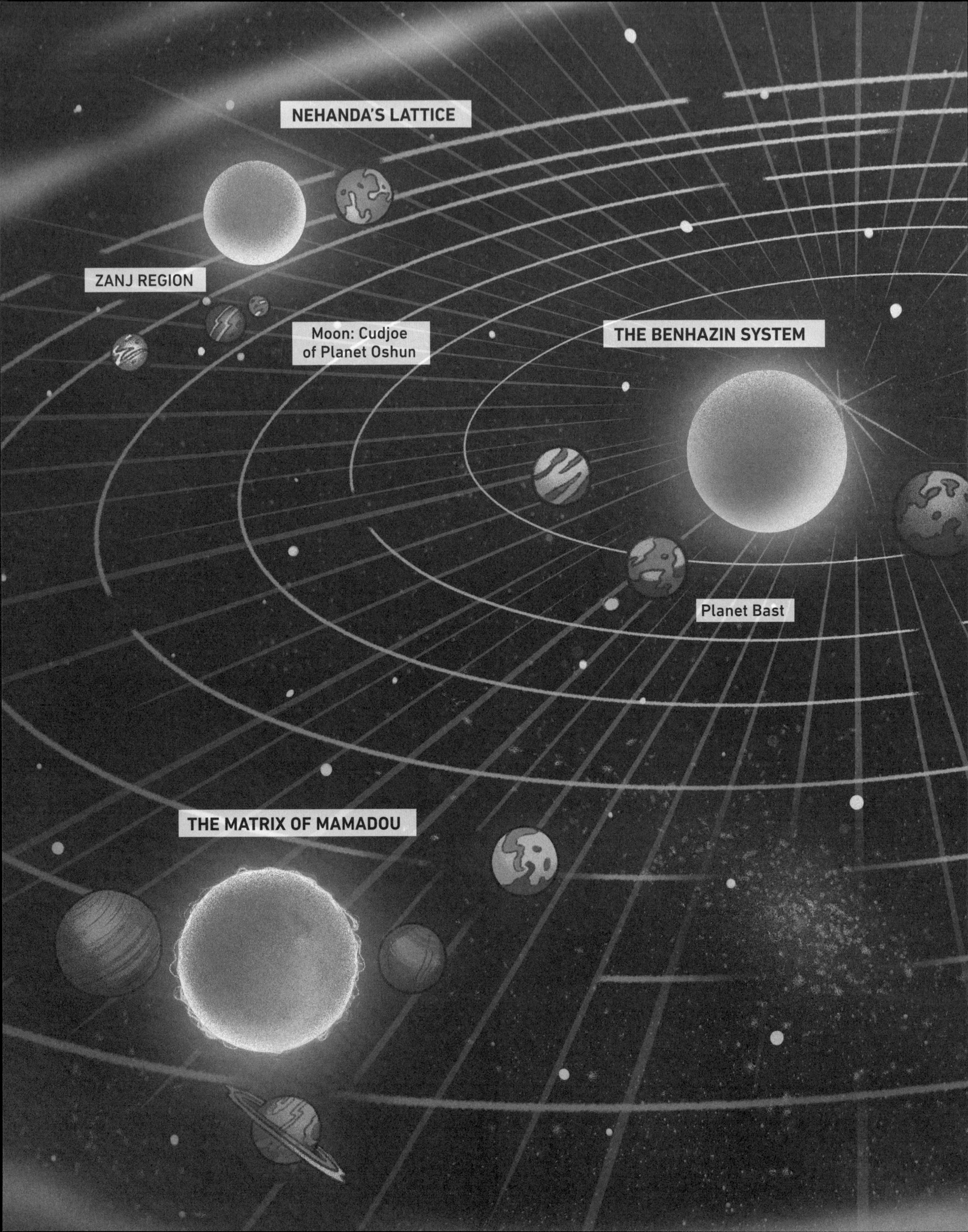
NEHANDA'S LATTICE
ZANJ REGION
Moon: Cudjoe
of Planet Oshun
THE BENHAZIN SYSTEM
Planet Bast
THE MATRIX OF MAMADOU

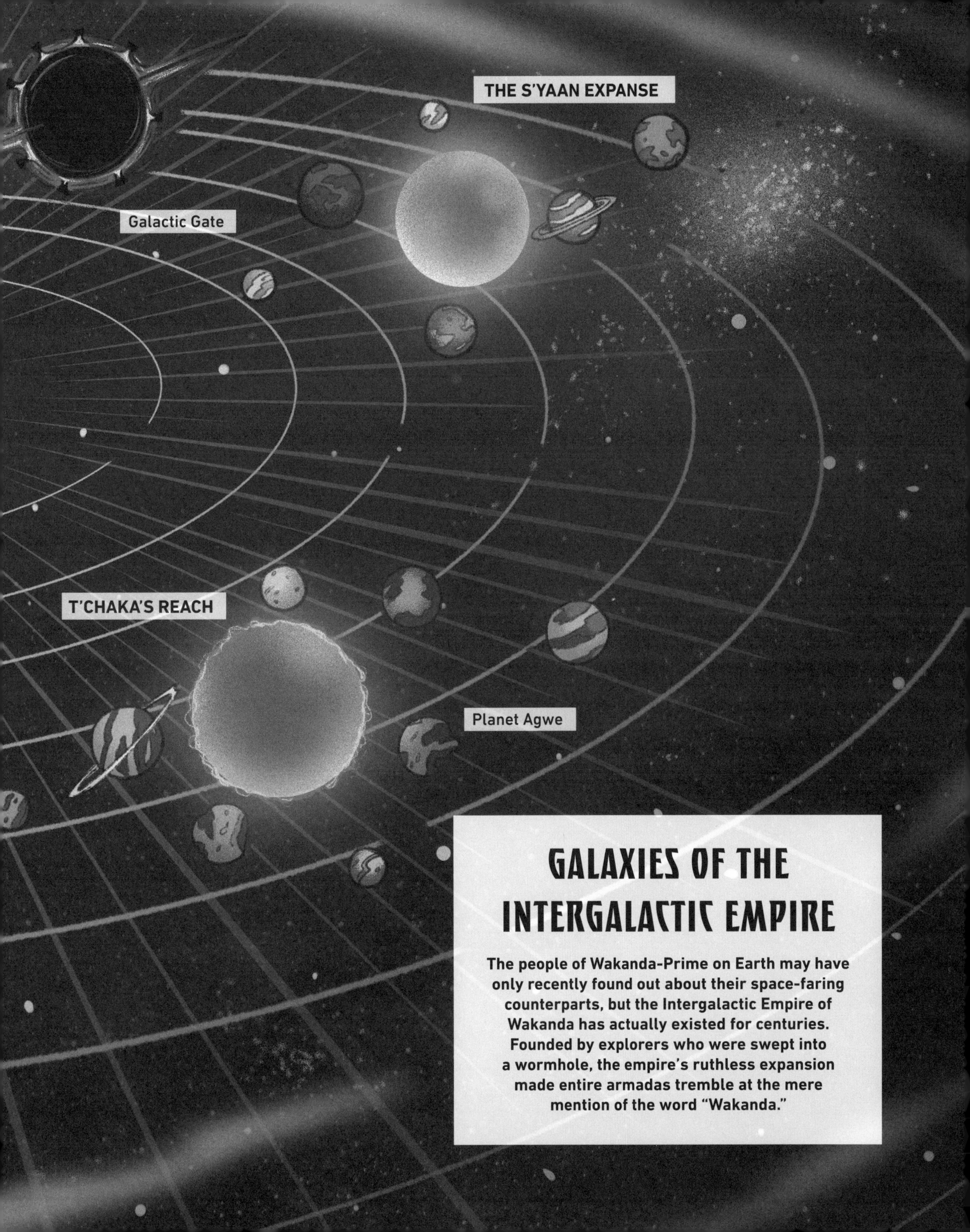

THE S'YAAN EXPANSE

Galactic Gate

T'CHAKA'S REACH

Planet Agwe

GALAXIES OF THE INTERGALACTIC EMPIRE

The people of Wakanda-Prime on Earth may have only recently found out about their space-faring counterparts, but the Intergalactic Empire of Wakanda has actually existed for centuries. Founded by explorers who were swept into a wormhole, the empire's ruthless expansion made entire armadas tremble at the mere mention of the word "Wakanda."

PLANET BAST

Planet Bast is the first world where time-lost Wakandans established as a settlement. It has become the throneworld of the Intergalactic Empire of Wakanda. The planet's name comes from the goddess Bast, who protected Wakanda in the deep past and has been worshipped by Wakandans for centuries. Bast's blessings help grant Wakandan rulers their superhuman abilities and the mantle of Black Panther.

Throne world
Planet Bast is the central hub of the Intergalactic Empire of Wakanda, from where all decrees and policies flow from.

T'Challa became a figure of legend to the people of the Intergalactic Empire.

Sentient beings from all over the empire's five galaxies make the pilgrimage to Bast to bask in imperial glory.

VIBRANIUM VECTORS

A group of Wakandan astronauts left Wakanda in search of vibranium. Their expedition led them to an interstellar sector rich in the super-metal. At first contact two millennia ago, the star system was ringed by a belt of asteroids made up of pure vibranium. The vibranium asteroid belt was eventually mined out of existence. The team settled on planet Bast and went on to conquer neighboring planets forging the Intergalactic Empire of Wakanda.

MERCENARY MOTIVATION

Commander N'Jadaka began his service to the Intergalactic Empire of Wakanda as a mercenary who led campaigns to conquer and colonize inhabited worlds in the surrounding solar systems. When N'Jadaka's popularity outstripped that of the emperor of planet Bast, the emperor and his advisors plotted to have N'Jadaka deployed on a mission that would lead to his death. Years later, a wormhole interfered with T'Challa's search for the lost astronauts, leaving him stranded in the Intergalactic Empire of Wakanda. The Empire's forces rescued and welcomed T'Challa at first, but threatened by the idea that the people of Bast might love the legendary hero more than him, N'Jadaka had T'Challa's mind erased and sent him to the far-off mines to work as a slave.

IMPERIAL ASCENSION

The emperor of planet Bast's plot to kill N'Jadaka backfired when N'Jadaka discovered and bonded with a Klyntar symbiote that granted him superhuman power. Upon his return to planet Bast, N'Jadaka assassinated the emperor and assumed the throne. Later, years into his reign, he attacked the panther goddess Bast and drained her of most of her godly essence. A weakened Bast would later hide inside the body of N'Jadaka's daughter Zenzi.

PLANET AGWE

After time-lost Wakandan astronauts landed on Planet Bast and laid the foundations for a new Intergalactic Empire of Wakanda, they colonized other nearby planets. These included the aquatic sphere of Agwe. Home to the amphibious Teku-Maza people, Agwe is a water world and was the location of a pivotal battle during the Maroon Rebellion.

Galactic flow
Sentient life on Planet Agwe stretches back eons, long before the founding of the Intergalactic Empire of Wakanda.

AQUATIC ANCESTRY

The bipedal Teku-Maza coexisted with massive whale-like creatures called Jengu, who were their evolutionary ancestors. As Wakandan Imperial forces enslaved the planet's humanoid inhabitants, they also hunted the Jengu to extinction. Despite their efforts, one sole remaining Jengu lived and held both races' ancestral history in its soul.

The Maroon rebels used special armor and weapons to fight Imperial forces in Agwe's war-torn waters.

"FROM THE JENGU, WE TEKU-MAZA EVOLVED INTO OUR CURRENT FORM. WE BUILT A GREAT CIVILIZATION BENEATH THE WAVES."

—Farouk, leader of the Maroon Rebellion

TIDES OF TURMOIL

A civil war rolled through Agwe's oceans after the Intergalactic Empire of Wakanda arrived and its Imperial forces attempted to seize control. Captain N'Yami eventually left Agwe and led the Maroon Rebellion that freed T'Challa from enslavement on planet Bast.

DEEP WATERS

Years into their fight with the Imperial forces, Captain N'Yami instructed Maroon general M'Baku of the Nameless, to enter into an alliance with Agwe's forces. However, unbeknownst to the Maroons, Agwe commander Jafari had a secret plan to sell them out to Imperial forces, and T'Challa and Maroon soldier Nakia found themselves imprisoned.

RECOVERED MEMORIES

During enslavement, Imperial forces stole and stored the memories of billions of sentient beings, including T'Challa. Teku-Maza rebels and the Maroons hatched a desperate plan to use the last Jengu to help T'Challa recollect his knowledge of self.

CELESTIAL SACRIFICE

With the rebels' plans to acquire the Jengu's repository of memories thwarted, Imperial forces descended on Agwe. After an incomplete evacuation, Agwe rebel leader Farouk made the fateful decision to detonate his planet's core and strike a fatal blow against the Empire. The resulting explosion martyred Farouk and the remaining Teku-Maza.

GALACTIC GATE

This outer space portal connects the Milky Way to the far-flung worlds of the Intergalactic Empire of Wakanda. The Galactic Gate's existence makes the kingdom of Wakanda one of the few nations on Earth with the capability to travel into deep interstellar space. This capability allows Black Panther to fight for justice all over the universe.

Express lane
Even with the lightspeed and space-fold technologies on many Imperial craft, it would take centuries to travel from Wakanda Prime to the systems of the Intergalactic Empire.

The space cruiser *Mackandal*, named after a legendary Haitian rebel fighter, was the Maroons' mobile base during the rebellion.

Maroon pilots flew smaller, more agile Zulu-class fighters in their battles against the Empire's forces.

A WAY BACK HOME

After the Jengu restored T'Challa's memories on Planet Agwe, T'Challa began working on a method to bridge the light years that separated him from his birth planet. He was successful in creating the Galactic Gate which led him home to Wakanda.

REVOLVING DOORS

After the symbiote harboring the soul of Imperial leader N'Jadaka stole away to Earth, it schemed to resurrect Killmonger with Tetu and Zenzi. T'Challa and his allies intervened, but were met by a deluge of Imperial troops coming through portals opened by their enemies.

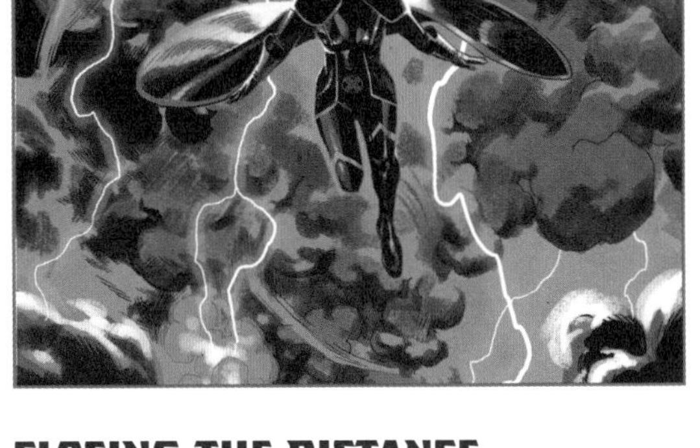

CLOSING THE DISTANCE

Even as T'Challa found his way back home, the war against Imperial forces continued to rage in deep space. The creation of the Galactic Gate meant that Wakanda was able to throw support to the Maroons in deep space. Storm helped turn the tide in one such battle, routing an entire squadron of Imperial fighters with her weather-controlling abilities.

RAPID TRANSIT

The Galactic Gate also provides passage to other distant star systems. Shuri, Manifold, and rebel leader M'Baku used it to travel to the heart of the rival Shi'ar Empire when Wakanda was asked to help thwart a cosmic crisis.

INDEX

N

O

P

Q

R

S

T

U

V

W

X

Z

Project Editor Pamela Afram
Senior Designer Clive Savage
Designers Lisa Robb, Jake Da'Costa
Production Editor Siu Yin Chan
Senior Production Controller Mary Slater
Managing Editor Emma Grange
Managing Art Editor Vicky Short
Publishing Director Mark Searle

Cover based on original design by Jake Da'Costa

DK would like to thank Cefn Ridout and Julia March for editorial help, Evan Narcisse for his text and expertise, Bex Glendining, Teo Georgiev, Shawn Martinbrough, and Adriano Lucas for their artwork, Sarah Singer, Wil Moss, and Jeff Youngquist at Marvel, and John Morgan III and Chelsea Alon at Disney Publishing. Special thanks to these creators who helped make Wakanda what it is: Daniel Acuña, Rich Buckler, Ta-Nehisi Coates, Billy Graham, Reginald Hudlin, Rian Hughes, Jack Kirby, Stan Lee, Don McGregor, Christopher Priest, and Brian Stelfreeze.

First American Edition, 2022
Published in the United States by DK Publishing, 1745 Broadway, 20th Floor, New York, NY 10019

DK, a Division of Penguin Random House LLC
22 23 24 25 10 9 8 7 6 5 4 3 2 1
001–326322–Sept/2022

Published in Great Britain by Dorling Kindersley Limited.

A catalog record for this book is available from the Library of Congress.
ISBN 978-0-7440-5030-1

Printed and bound in China

For the curious
www.dk.com

MIX
Paper | Supporting responsible forestry
FSC™ C018179